PREPARING
THE SECONDARY

BOOK 2
ENGLISH

Bell & Hyman · London

TEST 1
A. Reading
A DAY BEFORE HISTORY BEGAN

I will suppose myself born a thousand years before Noah was born or thought of. How shall I spend my day?

I rise with the sun and at once kneel to worship him. Then I prepare my breakfast; I swallow some goat's milk and a dozen good sizeable cakes.

After breakfast, I fasten a new string to my bow and, my youngest boy having played with my arrows till he has stripped off all the feathers, I find myself obliged to repair them. The morning is thus spent in preparing for the chase and it becomes necessary that I should dine.

What shall I have for dinner? I dig up my roots. I wash them and boil them. I find that they are not done enough; so I boil them again. This makes my wife angry; we dispute but soon settle the point. In the meantime the fire goes out and must be kindled again. All this is very amusing.

In the afternoon I hunt. I bring home my prey. With the skin of it I mend an old coat, or I make a new one.

By this time the day is far spent. I feel fatigued, and retire to rest. I am glad to say "*Good night!*"

Cowper (adapted)

1. Name the book in which we may all read about Noah.

2. What did the writer keep instead of a cow?

3. How many persons are mentioned in the story?

4. How did this hunter kill his prey?

5. What does the writer say instead of **hunting**?

6. How does the writer say **I have to mend them**?

7. Which of the following things could the writer **not** do:
    cook, sing, read or **dance**?

8. How do you know that he was a man?

9. What happens while the man and his wife are quarrelling?

10. How do you think the man could have lit his fire?

11. How does the writer say **tired**?

12. The animals which the man killed had two uses. What **were** they?

B. General

1. **I have a potato. Tom has a potato. So together we have two . . .** Write the missing word.
2. (*a*) **John ran well but came in 4th.** (*b*) **December is the 12th month of the year.** Write **4th** and **12th** as ordinary words.
3. Write with capital letters only where necessary:
   IT'S A LONG WAY TO TIPPERARY.
4. Copy the following and add any stops needed.
   Apples pears bananas grapes and oranges
5. Re-write with the necessary punctuation:
   Im ready sir she said
6. Change the masculine names into the corresponding feminines and re-write the following sentence:
   He was the King's son.
7. What do we call a shop-keeper who sells things such as:
   (*a*) tea, coffee, sugar, biscuits and rice;
   (*b*) medicines, ointments and pills?
8. **Permit** means nearly the same as which of the following:
   sift? by hand? allow? order? or try?
9. "Between you and . . ., it was quite wrong." Which word is missing?
   Me? Them? Her? I? or Us?
10. Form a word from **strong** that will complete the following sentence:
    Alan was a lad of great . . .
11. What word is needed to finish the sentence below:
    Bite a piece off and let me see how much you have b . . . ?
12. What is the opposite of (*a*) **agreeable** (*b*) **nonsense**?
13. Write the second sentence in full so that it agrees with the first:
    (*a*) Tom said, "I am coming." (*b*) Tom said that . . .
14. Re-arrange the following in alphabetical order:
    child, chief, cherub, canary, cement.
15. Choose the best of the words in brackets for finishing the following sentence:
    I noticed that the TV speaker spoke into the (megaphone, microphone, telephone, magneto).
16. Alec said he didn't feel up to the mark. Was he feeling:
    (*a*) Not quite ready? (*b*) Not very well?
    (*c*) Not beaten? **or** (*d*) Not quite finished?
17. Make the following two sentences into one:
    This is the house. Jack built it.
18. "He was as strong as a lion."
    Re-write the above beginning with the words, "His strength . . ."

TEST 2

A. Reading

BEWARE OF COWS!

People from the towns often amuse us in the country by running away from peaceful cows.

On one occasion we saw a man in a bowler-hat, grey-flannel suit, and white canvas shoes, solemnly sitting on a farm cart that had been left in a field. Apparently he had been walking across the field when some cows had taken an interest in him and wandered towards him. Terrified, he dashed for the nearest place of safety, and there we found him in the cart, looking like a picture from a comic paper.

He shouted at us to drive the cows away, but as he had no right to be in the field we left him sitting there until we drove the cows in for milking.

Cows are always inquisitive animals; if they see anything strange they always go to investigate. The other day our mare had a foal and when we turned it into the field the young cows became interested and walked round it, very curious to know what it was. They had never seen one before.

The mare was very angry with them. She put her ears back and neighing loudly she made short charges to chase them away. Now that the cows are used to the foal they graze near it without showing the slightest interest.

J. Farmer [by kind permission of the *Radio Times*.]

1. How many different things did the mare do to show that she was angry with the young cows?

2. Find a word in the story for **a mother horse**.

3. Find another word for a **baby horse**.

4. When the writer saw the man in the cart, what did it remind him of?

5. Which word is used that means **bite the grass and eat it**?

6. Which word in the story means **very curious**?

7. Which word in the story tells you that **the man in the bowler hat was scared**?

8. At what time of the day—morning, afternoon, evening or night—do you think the man in the bowler hat left the cart?

9. Find a word in the story which means **try to find out**.

10. Which word tells you that the writer was only guessing at the reason why the man in the bowler hat was sitting in the farm cart?

11. What name do we give to **a father horse**?

12. Find a word in the story for **the sound a horse makes**.

B. General
1. I am, Yours tr—y, John Smith.
   Write the unfinished word in full.
2. (a) One hundred years is called a . . . . What?
   (b) In which century are you living?
3. Re-write with capital letters where they are required:
   you may bring mary when you come to see us on monday.
4. Come here quickly; you will get wet there.
   What do you call the stop after **quickly**?
5. Re-write with the necessary punctuation:
   Go away at once she exclaimed
6. Change the masculine into the corresponding feminine words and re-write:
   I spoke to the gentleman's man-servant.
7. What do we call a shopkeeper who sells such things as:
   (a) rings, bracelets, necklaces and brooches;
   (b) knives, scissors and other cutting tools?
8. A **colleague** is which of the following? Is it a
   college friend? conspirator? fellow-worker? or goal-keeper?
9. Choose one of the words in the brackets to make the sentence correct:
   Who (**done, did, is done, didn't, done**) it?
10. Form a word from **miracle** to complete the following:
    The man's conjuring tricks seemed to be . . . .
11. What is the missing word below?
    Who drank the milk? Someone must have dr— it.
12. Write a phrase opposite in meaning to "**hide your ignorance**".
13. Re-write the following sentence beginning, "He said that:
    He says, "I will go" but he doesn't mean it.
14. Arrange in alphabetical order:
    centre, baker, butcher, arrival, break.
15. Which word in the brackets would you choose for finishing the following sentence?
    In order to tell whether the wall was upright the workmen used a (spirit-level, compass, plumb-line, meter).
16. **Henry is a bit of a rough diamond.** In other words he was
    (a) Bright and hard? (b) Worthy but not polite?
    (c) Valuable and rare? (d) Hard and rude?
17. Make a single sentence of the two that follow. Use the words **that was**.
    A bus was passing. The man held up his hand for it to stop.
18. "Leave two centimetres between the lines."
    Re-write this, beginning, "The space . . . .

TEST 3

A. Reading

HOW ROBINSON CRUSOE DRESSED HIMSELF
AFTER HIS SHIPWRECK

I had a great high, shapeless cap, made of a goat's skin, with a flap hanging down behind, as well to keep the sun from me as to shoot the rain off from running into my neck; nothing being so hurtful in these climates as the rain upon the flesh under the clothes. I had a short jacket of goatskin, the skirts coming down to about the middle of the thighs, and a pair of open-kneed breeches of the same. The breeches were made of the skin of an old he-goat, whose hair hung down such a length on either side, that it reached to the middle of my legs; stockings and shoes I had none, but had made me a pair of somethings, I scarce know what to call them, to flap over my legs, and lace on either side; but of a most barbarous shape as indeed were all the rest of my clothes. I had on a broad belt of goat's skin dried, which I drew together with two thongs of the same, instead of buckles, and on either side of this hung a little saw and a hatchet. I had another belt, not so broad, which hung over my shoulder; and at the end of it, under my left arm, hung two pouches, both made of goat skin, too, in one of which hung my powder, in the other my shot. At my back I carried my basket, on my shoulder my gun, and over my head a great clumsy, ugly goat-skin umbrella.

Daniel Defoe, Robinson Crusoe

1. Write down the names of five things which Robinson Crusoe took about with him which he did not make for himself.

2. What do you call the stops used after the words **neck, legs, side** and **shoulder**?

3. Write down three words which tell you that Robinson Crusoe's garments were not well made.

4. Robinson Crusoe's cap kept him safe from two things. What were they?

5. What word does the writer use instead of **leather strap**?

6. Name an animal that Robinson Crusoe must have killed.

7. "A pair of open-kneed breeches of the same." What was the **same**?

8. Down as far as what joints do you think that the hem of Crusoe's breeches reached when worn?

9. Have you anything to say about the length of Crusoe's jacket?

10. What were Crusoe's "somethings" meant to be?

B. General
1. **Can you play the piano? We have three p——s at our school.** Write the unfinished word in full.
2. **We learn about different countries in our . . . lessons.**
   Name the **subject** of these lessons.
3. Re-write with capital letters only where needed:
   Robert louis stevenson is the Author of Treasure island.
4. **It's a nice cake. Don't you think so?**
   Write the above in full without abbreviations.
5. Re-write with the necessary stops and quotation marks:
   Do you really think so John said.
6. Change the feminine names to the corresponding masculine names and re-write:
   The duchess was accompanied by her daughter.
7. What do we sometimes call the man who gets his living as the driver of a private motor car?
8. What is an **assault**? Is it a
   food for donkeys? performing animal? attack? or salt food?
9. Choose the right word in the brackets to complete the sentence:
   The child could not shout (**no, not more, any, more**) louder.
10. What word formed from **wise** is needed to complete:
    The aged statesman was a man of great . . .?
11. Write down the word formed from **eat** which is required at the end of the sentence that follows:
    Eat some lettuce and tell me when you have . . . it.
12. Add something to **modest** to make it opposite in meaning.
13. "May I leave early?" Jack asked.
    Rewrite this beginning, **Jack asked if . . .**
14. Arrange in alphabetical order:
    smoke, smear, smock, small, smack.
15. Which word in the brackets would best complete the following sentence?
    The doctor listened to my heart-beats through his . . . (barometer, microphone, stethoscope, megascope).
16. **Your friend looks down in the mouth.** Was he:
    (*a*) Suffering from toothache? (*b*) In poor health?
    (*c*) In low spirits? **or** (*d*) Open-mouthed?
17. Make the following two sentences into one, using the word **who**:
    A strange man appeared at the door. Mr Jones invited him inside.
18. "He rose to power in the thirteenth century."
    Re-write the above sentence, beginning, "His rise . . .

TEST 4
A. Reading
A SHEET OF NEWSPAPER

"I don't know where all this paper comes from," said Mother as she was tidying the kitchen up.

"You may not believe it," said Father, "but the newspaper I am reading was made, along with others of course, from a tree."

"Really!" I exclaimed.

"Yes," he replied. "We make furniture, as you know, from the trees that give us hardwood but millions of softwood trees are grown for the paper-makers. In Russia and Canada, thousands of men are employed in cutting down trees, sawing them into logs and then grinding down these logs into pulp ready for making into the kind of paper we call *newsprint*.

"I used to work as a boy in a paper-mill where paper was made," Father went on. "It was my job to fill up a large vat with all kinds of rag and waste paper. In this vat they were thoroughly cleaned and after that they were ground down into pulp and boiled in another vat. Three or four days afterwards the pulp was spread out in flat troughs and allowed to dry. Then it was rolled into sheets ready for those who wanted to buy it."

"I think I should like to work in a paper-mill," I said.

"Well," said Father, "there is a very nice factory not very far from here where they make the very best paper from a grass called Esparto grass that comes from Spain."

J. R. Crossland, *Plain English* [by kind permission of W. Collins, Sons, and Co., Ltd.]

1. What other kind of mill do you know of besides a paper-mill?
2. What name is given to a **tub** in this extract?
3. What kinds of tree are chosen to make newspaper pulp from?
4. In what countries are the logs ground down into pulp?
5. What else is paper made from besides wood-pulp?
6. Which of the following words rhymes with **trough**:
    bough, dough, enough, cough, though, rough, lough?
7. Name a country where you would expect to be able to buy plenty of the best paper.
8. What are the words used in this extract to express surprise?
9. How many things must be done before everything is ready for making newsprint? Name them.
10. How have you heard the word **pulp** used in some other way besides in paper-making?
11. How many paragraphs are there in the extract above?
12. Name three kinds of tree that give us hard wood for making furniture.

B. General

1. Tom had his bus fare. Mary had her bus fare. So both had th— bus fares.
   Write the unfinished word in full.
2. I was reading about Columbus in the 9th chapter of my book.
   Write 9th as an ordinary word.
3. The car was (*a*) station-ry outside the (*b*) station-r's.
   Write the unfinished words in full.
4. Show that you know the difference between **it's** and **its** by copying the following with any correction needed.
   Its a fine day for the swallow and its young.
5. Re-write with the necessary punctuation:
   Peter said to the policeman will you tell me the time please
6. Copy the following with masculines changed to the corresponding feminines:
   How can a bachelor be a widower?
7. What do we call people who kill others and eat their flesh?
8. To be **banished** is to be . . . what?
   Is it to be:
   sent away? stopped? made to disappear? disliked? or imprisoned?
9. Complete the following sentence by choosing the right word in the brackets:
   My mother (**teached, learned, learnt, taught**) me to read.
10. Form another word from **popular** that would complete the following sentence:
    He never gained any . . . as a teacher.
11. What is the unfinished word in the sentence that follows?
    I see that the bird has fl— away. I wonder where it *flew*.
12. Change (*a*) **behave** and (*b*) **believe** into their opposites by adding prefixes.
13. "Will you help me, Tom, to carry my box?" asked Mary.
    Re-write the above sentence beginning, Mary asked Tom . . .
14. Write down the vowels in **instantaneous** in the order in which they occur.
15. Which word is best of those in the brackets for finishing the following?
    The instrument used for forecasting the weather is the (**barometer, thermometer, radio set, dynamo**).
16. **Tell that to the Marines.** This means that what has been told you is—which?
    (*a*) A good story? (*b*) Something not to be believed?
    (*c*) A naval story? **or** (*d*) A riddle?
17. What word is needed to begin the following unfinished sentence?
    . . . I have begged him to come, he still refuses.
18. Re-write the following sentence, beginning, "The speech . . .
    "The Mayor spoke for forty minutes."

TEST 5
A. Reading
THE LION AND THE MOUSE

A lion was sleeping in his lair when a mouse, not knowing where he was going, ran over the mighty beast's nose and awakened him. The lion clapped his paw upon the frightened little creature, and was about to make an end of him in a moment when the mouse, in pitiable tone, besought him to spare one who had so unconsciously offended, and not stain his paws with so insignificant a prey. The lion, smiling at his little prisoner's fright, generously let him go.

Now it happened no long time after that the lion, while ranging the woods for his prey, fell into the toils of the hunters, and finding himself entangled without hope of escape, set up a roar that filled the whole forest with its echo. The mouse, recognising the voice of his former preserver, ran to the spot, and without more ado, set to work to nibble the knot that bound the lion, and in a short time set the noble beast at liberty.

This shows us that kindness is not always thrown away, and that the least among us may have it in his power to return a favour.

ÆSOP

1. What can we call the place where a lion rests besides a **den**?

2. How is the mouse spoken of besides by his name?

3. How does the writer say: **begged the lion to let off a creature who had not meant to do him any harm**?

4. What do you think that **the toils of the hunters** were made of?

5. What is meant by his **former preserver**?

6. How does the writer say **wasting no time**?

7. Find a word which means **tiny and unimportant**.

8. Whose **kindness** is spoken of in the last sentence?

9. Who returned a favour in the story?

10. What do we call those animals which are killed by the lion for food?

11. What word does the writer use for **voice** in the first paragraph?

12. What does the writer say for **a special kindness done to someone**?

B. General

1. Write the word beginning with **t** that rhymes with **rung** and **sung**.
2. What do we call the people who live in Holland?
3. Re-write properly: **cyprus is an Island in the mediterranean.**
4. Copy the following sentence adding stops where needed.
   Ive come to see you sir
5. Re-write with the necessary punctuation:
   Oh what fun we all exclaimed.
6. Change the masculine terms to the corresponding feminines and re-write:
   My brother has four buck rabbits.
7. If anything (like glass, for example) can be easily seen through we say that it is . . . what?
8. A person in **agony** is in what? Is it:
   disgrace? uncertainty? torment? defeat? or **prison?**
9. Which words in the brackets would you choose to complete this sentence?
   The dog **(laid, lay, layed, lied)** there all day with **(its, it's)** puppies.
10. Form other words from **quarrel** to complete the following sentences:
    (*a*) **Annie was always a . . . child.**
    (*b*) **She was really fond of q . . .**
11. Who drew this picture? One of you must have dr--- it.
    What is the unfinished word?
12. How is the opposite of **polite** formed? Write it.
13. "I have been naughty," the little girl said.
    Re-write the above beginning "The little girl said that . . .
14. Give the meaning of (*a*) C.O.D. (*b*) M.P.
15. Which word in the brackets best completes the following sentence?
    The hall had a seating (ability, capacity, power, capability) of five hundred.
16. "Don't you like blowing your own trumpet!" What does this mean?
    (*a*) Enjoying the music you make? (*b*) Boasting?
    (*c*) Making a noise? or (*d*) Exercising your lungs?
17. What word is best for completing the following sentence?
    John said he would come . . . we liked it or not.
18. "You need not explain your absence."
    Re-write the above sentence beginning, "No explanation . . .

TEST 6
A. Reading
KEEPING FOWLS

There are very few children who have not seen the principal kinds of poultry kept in this country: fowls, ducks, geese and turkeys. Fowls, of course, are the commonest kind to be seen. They are kept as a rule for the sake of their eggs which make an excellent food. A single hen will lay as many as one hundred and fifty eggs a year, the greatest number in April and May, and the fewest in November and December. Those who keep fowls feed them on corn or on a mash which consists of bran and barley meal mixed with a little oil.

The corner of a cottage garden is often railed off to make a chicken run. If you watch the hens, you will see them teaching the tiny chicks how to feed. The father bird seems to take no notice at all of the chicks, but he looks after the mother hen very well indeed.

The cock bird will scratch and dig up grubs and worms for his family, and when food is given to him, he will at once call the hens, and will not touch a morsel himself till they have finished eating.

He also keeps good order in his family, and should the hens quarrel, or the young cockerels spar and fight, he will strut up to them and quickly restore order. So you see that although the hen gives us the eggs we so much enjoy, the cock plays his part too, and plays it well.

1. What name do we give to fowls, ducks, geese and turkeys?

2. In which months of the year will hens lay eggs nearly every day?

3. Name three things put into a mash for chickens.

4. Which parent looks after the chickens and teaches them what to eat and how to eat it?

5. What is the father fowl called?

6. Name two kinds of food which fowls dig up in a garden.

7. What is a young cock fowl called?

8. Which word is often used to describe a father fowl's walk?

9. Which fowl takes his meals last?

10. Write down four words used as names for different kinds of fowl.

11. Which word is used as the name of a **very small amount**?

12. Which word in the extract means **chief**?

B. **General**
1. Did you forget the k——s, forks and d—s—t spoon when you l—d the table?
   Write the unfinished words in full.
2. Which day of the week follows Friday?
3. Which words would you write with capital letters in the following sentence?
   I read a book last week called tiger hunting.
4. Re-write correctly:
   (a) I had my little girls shoe mended.
   (b) This is not a mixed school but a girls school.
5. Re-write correctly:
   Tell me madam is this the way to the town hall I said.
6. Change feminines to the corresponding masculines and re-write:
   Will you let your aunt know that her niece is here?
7. The woman in charge of the work of a hospital is called the . . . What?
8. An inquisitive person is . . . What? Is he:
   fidgety? rude? vain? curious? or excited?
9. "He couldn't spend (nothing, anything) because he hadn't (no, any, not a lot of) money."
   Which words in the brackets would make this sentence correct :
10. Form a word from **generous** to complete the following:
    The colonel was noted everywhere for his . . .
11. I saw the moon rise yesterday; it has not r—— this evening yet.
    What is the unfinished word in the sentence above?
12. From the words (a) **regular** (b) **valuable** form their opposites.
13. "Do you know where my mother has gone?" said John to Anna.
    Re-write the above sentence beginning, John asked Anna if . . .
14. What words have the following as their shortened forms?
    bus, pram, phone and **prom.**
15. Which word in the brackets is best for finishing the following sentence?
    No one likes to see a dog (malcontent, maltreated, malleable, malevolent).
16. The thief showed them a clean pair of heels. What does this mean?
    (a) He ran away? (b) He took off his socks?
    (c) His shoes were clean? or (d) He had just washed his feet?
17. What single word would do for finishing the following sentence?
    Be careful . . . you should fall.
18. "You need not come unless you like."
    Re-write the above sentence, beginning, "There is . . .

TEST 7
A. Reading
DIVIDING THE JAM PUFF

The knife descended on the jam puff and cut it in two. But the result was not satisfactory to Tom, for he still eyed the halves doubtfully. At last he said,

"Shut your eyes, Maggie."

"What for?"

"You never mind what for. Shut them when I tell you."

Maggie obeyed.

"Now, which'll you have, Maggie—right hand or left?"

"I'll have the half without the jam," said Maggie, keeping her eyes shut to please Tom.

"Why, you don't like that, you silly. You may have it if it comes out to you fair, but I shan't give it to you unless it does. Right or left—you choose, now. Ha-a-a!" said Tom as Maggie peeped. "You keep your eyes shut, now, else you shan't have any."

Maggie cared less that Tom should have the utmost possible amount of puff than that he should be pleased with her for giving him the best bit. So she shut her eyes quite closed till Tom told her to say which, and then she said, "Left hand."

"You've got it," said Tom in rather a bitter tone.

"What! the bit without the jam?"

"No. Here, take it," said Tom firmly, handing the best bit to Maggie.

"Oh, please, Tom, have it. I don't mind—I like the other. Please take this."

"No, I shan't," said Tom.

George Eliot, *The Mill on the Floss* (adapted)

1. Which half of the jam puff was the "best half?"
2. Which half did Maggie want Tom to have?
3. What did Maggie do so that she should know how to answer Tom?
4. Why did Tom say "Shut your eyes, Maggie?"
5. Write "Shan't" as two words.
6. Which piece of jam puff did Tom hide in his left hand?
7. Which words tell you that Tom did not like Maggie getting the best half?
8. **Maggie obeyed.** What did Maggie do when she obeyed?
9. Which word tells you that Tom noticed that Maggie was peeping?
10. Which of the children would you call the unselfish one?

B. General

1. (a) B-l--ved (b) R-c--ved (c) Bes--ged (d) S--zed.
   Write in full the unfinished words, all of which contain either ie or ei.
2. This year is the c-------y of the great man's birth.
   Write the unfinished word in full.
3. I WENT TO THE REGAL CINEMA TO SEE RICHARD THE THIRD.
   Write the above sentence with capital letters only where needed.
4. Insert an apostrophe in the following sentence:
   The explosion spoilt the childrens clothes.
5. Re-write the following sentence correctly:
   Indeed he said do you know who I am.
6. Change feminines to the corresponding masculines and re-write:
   Her sister has become a nun.
7. What name do we give to a boy who enjoys frightening boys not so big or strong as he is himself?
8. What name do we give to the onlookers at a game?
9. Choose the correct words from the brackets to complete this sentence:
   Have you (see'd, saw, seen) John since he (gone, went, is going) away?
10. Form a word from give to complete the following sentence:
    Take the watch as a . . . from your Uncle John.
11. What are the unfinished words below? Write the sentence in full.
    Pract— makes perfect; therefore pract—.
12. Form its opposite from the word order.
13. **Ben thinks he can do as he likes.** Re-write this as follows:
    Sarah said that Ben . . . liked.
14. What is meant by the 10th inst?
15. Which of the following words in brackets best completes the sentence?
    Very few days are passed without some slight (mission, missive, mishap, misfit).
16. **The tribesmen decided to bury the hatchet.** What does this mean?
    (a) To hide it? (b) To try another tool?
    (c) To cease quarrelling? or (d) To put it into the coffin with their chief?
17. Re-write the following sentence using the word **through**:
    Henry was late for school because he lost his satchel.
18. "Thousands saw the mine explode."
    Re-write the above sentence, beginning, "The explosion . . .

TEST 8

A. Reading

LITTLE TOMMY AND THE LION

Here, then, were the lions. It was a fine sight to see nine or ten of these noble-looking animals lying down in various attitudes, quite indifferent apparently to the people outside their den, basking in the sun and slowly moving their tufted tails to and fro. William examined them at a respectable distance from the bars; and so did Tommy who had his mouth wide open with astonishment in which there was at first not a little fear mixed, but he soon got bolder. Tommy looked at the lions and then he wanted to make them move about. There was one fine full-grown young lion, about three years old, who was lying down nearest to the bars and Tommy took up a stone and threw it at him. The lion appeared not to notice it for he did not move, although he fixed his eyes on Tommy. So Tommy became more brave and threw another, and then another, approaching each time nearer to the bars.

All of a sudden the lion gave a tremendous roar and sprang at Tommy, bounding against the iron bars of the cage with such force that, had they not been very strong, it must have broken them. As it was they shook and rattled so that pieces of mortar fell out of the stones next to them. Tommy shrieked and fortunately for himself fell back and tumbled head over heels or the lion's paw would have reached him. He roared with fright as soon as he could fetch his breath while the lion stood at the bars, lashing his tail, snarling and showing his enormous fangs.

"Take me away," cried Tommy who was terribly frightened. "I won't throw any more stones, Mr Lion. I won't indeed."

Adapted from *Masterman Ready* (Capt. F. Marryat)

1. Why did Tommy throw the stones?
2. How many stones did he throw?
3. What do we call the home in which lions live?
4. Which words in the story are used for the **different ways** in which the lions lay resting?
5. Find the words which described Tommy's two kinds of feeling when he first saw the lion.
6. The lion showed his anger to Tommy in three ways. What were they?
7. How long does it take a lion cub to grow into a full-sized lion?
8. How does the writer say that William thought it wise not to go too near the cage?
9. Write down the words which mean that the lions **seemed to be completely unaware that anyone was looking at them**.
10. What made Tommy think that the lion had not seen him throw the first stone?

B. General

1. At the shallow end of the baths the water only reaches up to my w—.
   Write the unfinished word in full.
2. At my brother's school they do experiments in the . . . lessons.
   Which lessons are these?
3. Write in full: (*a*) Louis XIV (*b*) Henry V.
4. All's well that ends well. Write **all's** in full.
5. Re-write with the necessary punctuation.
   I wish Mary would come soon sighed her mother.
6. Change feminines into the corresponding masculines and re-write:
   The witch cast her spell on the princess.
7. What is the name given to a place in a desert where water is to be found?
8. What name do we give to people gathered together to listen to a concert?
9. Choose the correct words in the brackets for a good sentence:
   We were (**to, two, too**) late to see how much the river (**had rose, had risen, rose, had rised**).
10. Form a word from **deep** to complete the sentence:
    The young swimmer got out of his . . .
11. Re-write in full the following:
    In v—n we tried to stop the blood from her cut v—n.
12. Using the word **connect** write its opposite.
13. "May I come with you, father?" asked Nan.
    Re-write this beginning, Nan asked her father if . . .
14. Name the buildings in which the following are made.
    (*a*) **money** (*b*) **leather** (*c*) **cast iron.**
15. Choose the word in the brackets that best concludes the following:
    The girl sang the solo without a piano (accident, accompaniment, accent, assent).
16. "**You must mind your p's and q's.**" What does this mean?
    (*a*) Write carefully? (*b*) Make good p's and q's?
    (*c*) Don't lose them? **or** (*d*) Be careful how you behave?
17. Make a single sentence out of the following two sentences using the word **which (or who).**
    Jane has a dog. She is very fond of it.
18. "We shall celebrate our victory tomorrow."
    Re-write the above sentence, beginning, "The celebration . . .

TEST 9
A. Reading
UNDER SENTENCE OF EXECUTION

"It's—it's a very fine day!" said a timid voice at her side. She was walking by the White Rabbit, who was peeping anxiously into her face.

"Very," said Alice: "Where's the Duchess?"

"Hush! Hush!" said the Rabbit in a low hurried tone. He looked anxiously over his shoulder as he spoke and then raised himself upon tiptoe, put his mouth close to her ear and whispered, "She's under sentence of execution."

"What for?" said Alice . . .

"She boxed the Queen's ears—" the Rabbit began. Alice gave a little scream of laughter.

"Oh! Hush!" the Rabbit whispered in a frightened tone. "The Queen will hear you."

Lewis Carroll, The Adventures of Alice in Wonderland.

1. "She was walking . . ." **Who** was walking?

2. The Rabbit was frightened. Which word describes Alice:
   nervous, excited, scared or **curious?**

3. Why did the Rabbit say "Hush! Hush!"?

4. Write the following in full: **Where's; it's.**

5. Why did the writer write **Queen's** and not **Queens'**?

6. Write down the words that mean:
   "**She has been condemned to death.**"

7. Do you know what the husband of a Duchess is called? What is it?

8. Instead of **looking anxiously** the writer could have written **looking with anx—**. Write the last word in full.

9. Form a word from **timid** (not **timidness**) to finish the following:
   The rabbit is known for its tim—

10. Finish this sentence:
    Alice was amused to think that . . .

11. One word in the passage above would **not** have been written if the rabbit had been as tall as Alice. Which is it?

12. What did Alice ask the Rabbit to tell her?

B. General

1. G—s which hand the penny is con——d (= hidden) in.
   Write the unfinished words in full.
2. Water, milk, ink and lemonade are all . . . what?
3. DO YOU SELL FRENCH WINE OR DANISH BUTTER?
   Re-write with as few capitals as possible.
4. I shan't let you. Oh, won't you!
   Write shan't and won't in full.
5. Re-write correctly:
   Beware I shouted theres a lion about.
6. What are the young ones of the following called?
   (*a*) bear (*b*) goose (*c*) dog.
7. By what name does a teacher refer to the children he teaches?
8. What name do we give to the people gathered together
   (*a*) **at a church service?**
   (*b*) **in a disorderly crowd?**
9. Choose the correct word in the brackets to make a good sentence:
   I asked her (**what, which, who**) boy came with her.
10. Form a word from **energy** to complete the following:
    Mollie was an . . . young woman.
11. Re-write the following with one word only from each bracket:
    No sooner had she (began, begun) to row than the boat (sunk, sank).
12. Using the words (*a*) **screw** (*b*) **judge** write their opposites.
13. "I hate you," said Philip to Susan.
    Re-write with **said that** in the sentence.
14. Where are the following kept?
    (*a*) cows (*b*) planes (*c*) books.
15. Which word in the brackets is best for finishing the following sentence?
    The lodger was (excused, accused, miscued, misused) of robbing his landlady.
16. "**Mary let the cat out of the bag.**" What did she really do?
    (*a*) Let the cat loose? (*b*) Forget to fasten the bag?
    (*c*) Feel sorry for the cat? or (*d*) Give away a secret?
17. Make a single sentence from the following two.
    The animal howls all night. It's the man's next door.
18. "You must choose wisely if you are to win."
    Re-write the above sentence, beginning, "A wise choice . . .

TEST 10
A. Reading
THE WIND IN A FROLIC

The wind one morning sprang up from sleep,
Saying, "Now for a frolic! Now for a leap!
Now for a madcap galloping chase!
I'll raise a commotion in every place!"
So it swept with a bustle right through a great town,
Cracking the signs and scattering down
Shutters, and whisking with merciless squalls
Old women's bonnets and gingerbread stalls.
There never was heard a much lustier shout
As the apples and oranges trundled about;
And the urchins that stand with their thievish eyes
For ever on watch, ran off with a prize.

Then it rushed like a monster on cottage and farm,
Striking their dwellers with sudden alarm;
And they ran out like bees in a midsummer swarm;
There were dames, with their kerchiefs tied over their caps,
To see if their poultry were free from mishaps;
The turkeys they gobbled, the geese screamed aloud,
And the hens crept to roost in a terrified crowd.

But the wind had swept on, and had met in a lane
With a schoolboy who panted and struggled in vain,
For it tossed him and twirled him, then passed, and he stood
With his hat in a pool and his shoes in the mud.

William Howitt, *Collected Poems*

1. How does the poet say: **Now for some fun**?
2. Would you say that the wind in the poem was a **hurricane**, a **breeze**, a **blizzard** or a **gale**?
3. Find the name used in the poem for a **sudden gust of wind**.
4. What did the small boys run off with as a prize?
5. How did the old ladies keep their caps on in the wind?
6. **Cracking the signs.** What signs would these be?
7. Find a word in the poem for **turkeys, geese** and **hens**.
8. Complete these sentences with words from the poem:
    (*a*) You do not see boys . . . their hoops as often as they once did.
    (*b*) The cow kept . . . her tail to drive the flies off her back.
9. Which words in the poem mean:
    (*a*) made a fuss and noise;
    (*b*) cried out?
10. Which phrase of three words in the poem means **safe** and **sound**?

B. General

1. "Here is a w----ing machine. Let us see who is the h-----r, you or --."
   Write the missing words in full.
2. What word beginning with c rhymes with **off**?
3. Which **word** in the following could have a capital letter besides the first word in the following sentence?
   In the spring they went away in the autumn they returned.
4. Re-write in full:
   You'll have to tell all that's oc—r-d.
5. Re-write correctly:
   Ah she cried there you are at last.
6. What are the young of the following called?
   (a) eagle (b) hare (c) mare.
7. The kind of doctor who devotes his time to performing operations is called a . . . what?
8. An **annual** holiday is one that takes place:
   In the summer? At week ends? Every year? or When factories close down?
9. "Here is the man (**who's, whose, shoes**) money has been (**took, tooked, taken**)."
   Write down the words you would choose to make a correct sentence.
10. Form a word from **proud** to complete the following:
    You should take a . . . in your appearance.
11. What should be the last word on the line below?
    Have you some matches? No, I haven't . . .
12. Form words that are opposite in meaning from (a) **legal** (b) **interested**.
13. "I saw you yesterday," said Steve.
    Re-write the above with the words **said that** in the sentence.
14. What would you expect to find in the following?
    (a) caddy (b) scabbard (c) wardrobe (d) scuttle.
15. Which word in the brackets is best for finishing the following sentence?
    I call a person who smokes twenty cigarettes a day an (**addict, adobe, adult, advowson**).
16. "**Don't rub me up the wrong way.**"
    This means, "Don't . . . What?
    (a) Annoy me? (b) Spoil my hair? (c) Tickle me? **or** (d) Be rough with me?
17. Make the following sentences into one sentence:
    They discovered a cave. It led them deep into the cliff.
18. "The two cars seemed bound to collide."
    Re-write the above sentence, beginning, "A collision . . .

TEST 11
A. Reading
HE DESERVED WHAT HE GOT

One day, when John and I had been out on some business for our master, and were returning gently on a long straight road, at some distance we saw a boy trying to leap a pony over a gate. The pony would not take the leap, and the boy cut him with a whip, but the pony only turned off on one side; he whipped him again, but the pony turned off on the other side.

When we were nearly at the spot, the pony put down his head, threw up his heels, and sent the boy neatly over a broad quickset hedge; and with the rein dangling from his head, he set off home at a full gallop. John laughed out quite loudly. "Serve him right," he said.

"Oh! oh! oh!" cried the boy, as he struggled out amongst the thorns; "I say, come and help me out."

"Thank ye," said John, "I think you are quite in the right place; and may be a little scratching will teach you not to leap a pony over a gate that is too high for him"; and with that John rode off.

Anna Sewell, Black Beauty

1. How many persons are mentioned in the story? (It is Black Beauty, a horse, who is supposed to be telling the story.)

2. What do you call the stop which is used in the story after the following words:
   (a) **one side** (b) **quickset hedge** (c) **thorns** and (d) **high for him?**

3. Why did the pony refuse to take the leap?

4. How was it that John was able to see the boy and the pony **at some distance**?

5. Why did the pony **turn off** to one side instead of leaping over the gate?

6. A quickset hedge is a hawthorn hedge. What did the hedge contain that hurt the boy?

7. What did the boy let go of when he was sent over the hedge?

8. What is usually said instead of **ye**?

9. Why do you think that John would not help the boy?

10. "Serve him right!" Serve **whom** right?

11. What do you think the pony's master might say when he saw his pony arrive home that day?

12. "And **with that** John rode off." With **what**?

B. General

1. **Tom rolled up his shirt sleeves to show us his mus—s.**
   Write the unfinished word in full.
2. Write the following sentence in full:
   The visitors pr-c—ded towards the Town Hall, pr-c-ded by a brass band.
3. LAST SATURDAY WE WENT TO LONDON FOR THE DAY.
   Which words would you write with capital letters in the above sentence?
4. **Can't you see where you're going?**
   Write **can't** and **you're** in full.
5. Re-write correctly:
   If its hot mother said you can take your coat off.
6. What are the young ones called that, when they are grown up, become:
   (*a*) frogs (*b*) birds (*c*) eels?
7. Name the kind of building which contains instruments for looking at the stars and studying them.
8. "I find your behaviour **intolerable**."
   Intolerable means: (*a*) **disgusting**? (*b*) **rude**? (*c*) **unbearable**? or (*d*) **annoying**?
9. Choose the words in brackets that make a correct sentence:
   Will they let (**you and me, you and I, I and you, we two**) go together?
10. Form a word from **variety** to complete the following sentence:
    There are . . . ways of getting to Oxford from here.
11. **We had just (give, gave, given) the sign when the bell (ring, rang, rung).**
    Re-write the above sentence with one word only from each bracket.
12. Using the word **rust** write a word opposite to it in meaning.
13. "We haven't seen you lately," said Will.
    Re-write the above with the words **said that** in the sentence.
14. **Aquiline** means like an eagle. What are the words ending in -ine that mean:
    (*a*) like an ass (*b*) like a dog (*c*) like a cat?
15. Choose the best word in the brackets for completing the following sentence:
    This sticking plaster is not very (adherent, admitted, adhesive, adjacent).
16. "I didn't expect them to throw cold water on my plans." This means which:
    (*a*) Cool them? (*b*) Drown them? (*c*) Try them out? **or** (*d*) Discourage me?
17. Make one sentence from the following two without using **and** or **so**:
    Father wore a green linen shirt. He walked on our right.
18. "The manager suggested that the two men should change jobs."
    Re-write the above sentence, beginning, "A change of job . . .

TEST 12

A. Reading

A BUNCH OF BANANAS

The most important fruit in Jamaica is one which you and I know very well. It is the banana. The banana plant is at least three metres high. It has a very thick stem from the top of which grow huge leaves. The bananas themselves grow in a huge cluster with the fruit pointing upwards. The fruit comes from a giant flower. The spike of this flower is the stem upon which the bananas grow.

It takes three men to cut a bunch of bananas. One man has a long pole with a fork at the end of it. He puts this against the bunch of fruit to prevent it from falling down. Then another man with a sharp cutlass makes a notch in the stem just below the bunch of fruit. The stem begins to bend, and the man with the pole slowly lowers the fruit until the third man can get it on his shoulder. Then the chopper chops through the stem and the bunch of bananas is carried away.

An ordinary bunch of bananas may be one and a half metres long and contain one hundred and fifty bananas. One bunch is almost as much as one man can carry. The bananas are usually cut while they are green and carried to cool storehouses to be kept until the steamers fetch them away.

B. G. Hardingham, V50–51, *Foundations of Geography* [by kind permission of Thomas Nelson & Sons, Ltd.]

1. Name a place where bananas grow.

2. To what height do banana plants grow?

3. About how many bananas grow in a bunch together?

4. How long is an ordinary bunch of bananas?

5. How many men does it take to cut a bunch of bananas?

6. In what way are the bananas different when they are cut from when they are eaten?

7. What is the cutting tool called which is used in cutting down the bananas?

8. How many men does it take to carry a bunch of bananas?

9. Find two words in the extract which mean **very big**.

10. On which part of the banana flower does the fruit grow?

11. Find a word in the extract meaning **bunch**.

12. The bananas do not grow like **grapes**. How **differently** do they grow?

B. General

1. **I couldn't understand them; they were speaking in a foreign lang—e.**
   Write the unfinished word in full.
2. Julius Caesar came to Britain in 55 B.C. What is meant by 55 B.C.?
3. I wrote an essay called **a day on a desert island** and used four capital letters. What did I actually write?
4. **Im sure theyre right.** Re-write this with the necessary punctuation.
5. Copy the following with the quotation marks and capitals needed:
   All I could say was good gracious.
6. What do the following grow from (or out of)?
   (*a*) bees (*b*) butterflies (*c*) toads.
7. Write the unfinished words in full:
   Henry was v--g--- about the date of the Great Pl--g--.
8. Which of the following should know most about illnesses?
   A physician? a physicist? a chemist? a nurse? or a surgeon?
9. Find a word to fill the blank below and write it in your book.
   I say, Tom, . . . I come with you?
10. Form a word from **strong** to complete the following sentence:
    Can you suggest a way of . . . this handle?
11. Re-write the following sentence with one word only from each bracket.
    The man who had (stole, stolen, steal) the lady's purse was (took, taken, take) prisoner.
12. Using the word **noble** form its opposite.
13. John told me not to make myself miserable thinking of it.
    Re-write the above beginning, John said, ". . .
14. Write the meanings of the following:
    (*a*) leonine (*b*) equine (*c*) bovine and (*d*) ovine.
15. Which word in the brackets would best finish this sentence?
    For three of us half a dozen sandwiches and some apples should be (addled, admixed, adequate, adjourned).
16. **The lads took French leave.** This means that they:
    (*a*) Had a holiday in France? (*b*) Went off without permission?
    (*c*) Got work in France? **or** (*d*) Took the French kind of leave?
17. Make the following two sentences into one without using **and** or **so**.
    The beggar was barefooted. I offered him some old shoes.
18. "Finish your work, boys, before midnight," we said.
    Re-write the above sentence beginning, "Our order was that . . .

TEST 13
A. Reading
AN EXCITING MOMENT

How long I slept I cannot tell, but I was suddenly awakened by one of the most tremendous roars I ever heard. It was so close to me, that in the confusion of my sleepy brain, it seemed to be far more terrible than that even of the Gorilla. I was mistaken in this, however, and no doubt my semi-somnolent condition tended to increase its awfulness.

Springing into a sitting posture, and by an involuntary impulse, reaching out my hand for my gun, which lay close beside me, I beheld a sight that was calculated to appal the stoutest heart. A lion of the largest size was in the very act of springing over the bushes and alighting on the zebra, which, as I have said, lay on the other side of the fire, and not four yards off from us. As the light glared in the brute's eyes, and, as it were, sparkled in gleams on its shaggy mane which streamed out under the force of its majestic bound, it seemed to my bewildered gaze as though the animal were in the air almost above my head and that he must inevitably alight upon myself. This, at least, is the impression left upon my mind now that I look back upon that terrific scene; but there was no time for thought. The roar was uttered, the bound was made, and the lion alighted on the carcass of the zebra almost in one and the same moment. I freely confess that my heart quailed within me. Yet that did not prevent my snatching up my gun; but before I had time to cock it the crashing report of Jack's elephant rifle almost split the drum of my ear, and I beheld the lion drop as if it had been a stone. It lay without motion, completely dead.

R. M. Ballantyne, The Gorilla Hunters

1. Name four animals mentioned.
2. By which of these animals was the writer awakened?
3. What does the writer say for his **half-awake state**?
4. The writer reached for his gun without thinking of what he was doing. Write down the phrase of four words which tells you this.
5. Which word in the passage reminds you that the lion is often called the king of beasts?
6. Find a word to describe how things happen that cannot be prevented.
7. Three things are described as happening all at once. Which was the **first** of the three events? Write down the words that describe it.
8. How does the writer say that **he was afraid**?
9. What does the writer say for **I saw something**?
10. "That did not prevent my snatching up my gun." What did not prevent it?

B. General

1. Tell Tom I must have a d-f-n—e reply by tomorrow.
   Write the unfinished word in full.
2. The exhibition was opened by H.R.H. the Duke of Edinburgh.
   What is the meaning of H.R.H.?
3. Here are three sentences. Which are the words that need capital letters?
   go into the garden and ask tom to pick some beans tell him to leave the smallest to grow
4. Where theres a will theres a way.
   Re-write the above with correct punctuation.
5. Copy the following but add the necessary quotation marks.
   Open your mouth said the doctor now keep quite still
6. What are the **two** parents of each of the following called?
   (a) lamb (b) duckling.
7. What do we call the chief officer of a navy?
8. "That is some consolation," said the man. **Consolation** means:
   Reward? Payment? Advice? or Comfort?
9. How would you finish the following?
   John is tall but I think that Peter is t-----.
10. Form a word from **hero** to complete the following:
    The young airman was already famous for his . . .
11. Write the unfinished word in full:
    We shall beat them tomorrow as we have always b—— them in the past.
12. Using the word **pleasure** make a word opposite to it in meaning.
13. **They told me that the manager would soon be back.**
    What did they actually say?
14. What name would you give to the following?
    Cottage, house, bungalow, mansion but not cinema.
15. Which of the words in brackets is best for finishing the following?
    Babies are not (admired, addressed, added, admitted).
16. **The man decided to throw up the sponge.** In other words he decided to do—which?
    (a) Try his luck? (b) Give in? (c) Get rid of the sponge? **or** (d) Say no more about it?
17. Make a single sentence from the following three sentences:
    The general passed by. The wounded soldier tried to stand up to salute him. The general didn't see him.
18. "We were all struck by his noble appearance."
    Re-write the above sentence beginning, "The nobility . . .

TEST 14
A. Reading
A SURPRISE VISIT AND A HURRIED DEPARTURE

The captain spun round on his heel and fronted us.

"Come Bill, you know me; you know an old shipmate, Bill, surely," said the stranger.

The captain made a sort of gasp.

"Black Dog!" said he.

"And who else?" returned the other.

"Now, look here," said the captain; "you've run me down; here I am. Well, then, speak up; what is it?"

Black Dog bade me go, and leave the door wide open.

"None of your keyholes for me, sonny," he said; and I left them together, and retired into the bar.

For a long time, though I did my best to listen, I could hear nothing but a low gabbling; but at last the voices began to grow higher, and I could pick up a word or two, mostly oaths, from the captain.

"No, no, no, no, and an end of it!" he cried once. And again, "If it comes to swinging, swing all, I say."

Then all of a sudden there was a tremendous explosion of oaths and other noises—the chair and table went over in a lump, a clash of steel followed, and then a cry of pain, and the next instant I saw Black Dog in full flight, and the captain hotly pursuing, both with drawn cutlasses, and the former streaming blood from the shoulder. Just at the door, the captain aimed at the fugitive one last tremendous cut, which would certainly have split him to the chine had it not been intercepted by our big signboard of Admiral Benbow. You may see the notch on the lower side of the frame to this day.

The blow was the last of the battle. Once out upon the road, Black Dog, in spite of his wound, showed a wonderful clean pair of heels, and disappeared over the edge of the hill in half a minute. The captain, for his part, stood staring at the signboard like a bewildered man. Then he passed his hand over his eyes several times, and at last turned back into the house.

R. L. Stevenson, *Treasure Island*

1. Why did Black Dog **ask** for the door to be left open? Give the **true** reason.
2. In what sort of house did the two men meet?
3. How does Admiral Benbow come into the story?
4. Find the word used by the writer for **swear-words**.
5. Which left the house first, the boy, the captain or the stranger?
6. From which man was the **cry of pain** heard?
7. "The former streaming blood." Who was "the former"?
8. Find a word which means a **person running away**.
9. The writer uses an old word which means **backbone**. Can you find it?
10. Something got in the way when the captain lashed out at Black Dog with his cutlass. What was it?

B. General
1. Harry took his mother's needlework s—s-rs to cut his nails.
   Write the unfinished word in full.
2. Write the word beginning with **d** that rhymes with **so.**
3. Which of the two words, grandmother, in the sentences below would you write with a capital letter.
   (*a*) When grandmother calls answer at once.
   (*b*) They all said she was a good grandmother.
4. Twas in Trafalgar Bay.
   Re-write the above correctly.
5. How would you write the following to gain full marks?
   Say ninety nine that was what the doctor said
6. What are the two parents of each of the following called?
   (*a*) Chicken (*b*) Cygnet.
7. If you know it, write the American name for **Autumn.**
8. "The book-keeper was negligent in her duties." **Negligent** means:
   Hardworking? Punctual? Careless? or Dishonest?
9. Write in your book the word which is unfinished below:
   There he was l—g on his back on the grass.
10. Form a word from **magic** to complete the following sentence:
    When the lights were lit the effect was . . .
11. **Come out from the bush. I can see where you have (hid, hided, hidden) yourself.**
    Which word in the brackets is required in the above.
12. What is the word opposite in meaning to **normal**?
13. **Ann said that she thought that she would be able to go.**
    What did Ann actually say?
14. What name would you give to the following?
    daffodil, tulip, narcissus, crocus but not primroses or violets.
15. Which word in the brackets is best for completing the following sentence?
    I can begin on Monday next if you are (advised, agreeable, alert, awake).
16. What is meant by **throwing dust in a person's eyes?** Is it:
    (*a*) Being mischievous? (*b*) Harming his eyesight?
    (*c*) Annoying him? or (*d*) Deceiving him?
17. Make a single sentence of the following using the word **that**:
    The troops came to a beautiful mansion. It was standing empty and desolate.
18. "The secretary undertook to organize the party."
    Re-write the above sentence, beginning, "The organization . . .

TEST 15

A. Reading

AN ADVENTURE WITH ELEPHANTS

Day had just broken, fresh and sparkling, and every leaf and blade of grass was twinkling with dew. A loud rumble sounded behind them and then a grating squeal. Kilango drew Jerogi back to the shelter of the tree trunk.

The next instant a bull elephant, its large ears outspread like two big leather fans, pushed its way through the bamboo thickets. It reached for a young shoot, growing high up, and snapped it off with a sharp report.

It went slowly, almost casually, making no noise as it moved. Only the snapping of the bamboos and the loud rumbling of the elephant's stomach told of its presence. As it walked away, the boys picked up their loads and followed at a cautious distance. The path along which it moved gradually sank down into a bog.

"It's lucky that we didn't go any further last night," laughed Jerogi, as the great beast suddenly splashed into the muddy waste.

They hung back for a few minutes and then walked slowly forward to see what the elephant was doing. Peering round a clump of cedars, they saw, to their astonishment, a large swamp enclosed by the forest trees, and in it playing and bathing in the mud some eighty to a hundred elephants. Some sat and wallowed in the black shining mud and squirted it over one another. Others lay peaceful and brooding while little red-beaked tick-birds searched for ticks in the thick, grey wrinkles of their skin. A cow elephant, with her babies, came to the water's edge to drink. Two elderly beasts sparred playfully, the clash of their ivory tusks mingling with the squeals of the excited babies.

M. C. Borer, *Kilango* [by kind permission of Sir Isaac Pitman & Sons Ltd.]

1. Which of the following would make the best title of the extract: "A Miraculous Escape", "An Amusing Adventure", "A Muddy Waste", "Elephants at Play"?
2. Which words in the third paragraph might seem to you to be untrue?
3. Find a phrase of two words which suggest that the bull elephant hardly seemed to care where it was going.
4. Find two other ways of describing the **muddy waste**.
5. Write down the names of the two trees mentioned.
6. Name three kinds of living creatures (besides the boys) mentioned.
7. How does the writer say that **two of the older elephants pretended to fight one another**?
8. How did the elephant reach the young bamboo shoot **growing high up**?
9. When the boys saw the elephants together were they hiding behind one tree or several trees? Write down the phrase that tells you.
10. What is a mother elephant called in the extract?

B. General

1. (a) This butter is g—r–nt--d to be pure.
   (a) Take this h—k—ch—f and wipe your eyes.
   Write the unfinished words in full.
2. Find two different opposites of more, one for each sentence:
   (a) More than a gram.
   (b) More than fifty came.
3. Re-write the following sentence with capitals only where they are required:
   THE LARGEST CITY IN THE BRITISH ISLES IS LONDON.
4. I thought he was in soldiers uniform.
   Re-write **soldiers** correctly.
5. How many paragraphs would you make of the following?
   Good said John rotten said Tom O.K. said Harry.
   Now copy the conversation with proper punctuation.
6. Re-write, changing the feminines to the corresponding masculines:
   The heiress to the throne is her niece.
7. What name do we give to goods sent out of the country by sea or air?
8. "The **benevolent** old gentleman had passed on." Benevolent means:
   Aged? Handsome? Polite? Kind-hearted? or Good-tempered?
9. Choose and write out the words in the brackets that are needed to make a correct sentence:
   I have fallen down and (**hurt, hurted**) my leg; I think I have (**broke, broken, breaked**) a bone in it.
10. Form a word from **trouble** to complete the following sentence:
    Dick has not been a . . . boy so far.
11. Re-write the following correctly with one word only from each bracket:
    Give her a (piece, peace) of cake and leave her in (piece, peace).
12. Change the word **merciful** to give it an opposite meaning.
13. "Do you think I shall be better soon?" I asked him.
    Re-write the above, beginning, I asked him whether . . .
14. What name would you give to the following:
    Gold, silver, copper, lead but not slate?
15. Which word in brackets would best complete the following sentence?
    Pores are tiny (apogees, apostles, aperients, apertures) in the skin.
16. What is meant by **smelling a rat**? Is it:
    (a) Nosing about like a dog? (b) Having a bad smell? (c) Thinking something is wrong? or (d) Expecting rats?
17. Make the following sentences into one, using the word **which**.
    She returned hurriedly to the cottage. She lived in it.
18. "The wedding was a splendid one, as everyone admitted."
    Re-write the above, beginning, "The splendour . . .

TEST 16
A. Reading
AN OLD SEAMAN

Besides the captain of the ship and the two men at the wheel, there were two other persons on deck; one was a young lad about twelve years old, and the other a weather-beaten old seaman, whose grisly locks were streaming in the wind as he paced aft and looked over the taffrail of the vessel.

Masterman Ready, for such was his name, had been more than fifty years at sea, having been bound apprentice to a collier which sailed from South Shields when he was ten years old. His face was browned from long exposure, and there were deep furrows on his cheeks, but he was still a hale and active man. He had served many years on board a man-of-war, and had been in every climate; he had many strange stories to tell, and he might be believed even when his stories were strange, for he would not tell an untruth. He could navigate a vessel, and, of course, he could read and write; he had read his Bible over and over again. The name of Ready was very well suited to him for he was seldom at a loss, and in cases of difficulty and danger, the captain would not hesitate to ask his opinion, and frequently take his advice. He was on board as second mate of the vessel.

Captain Frederick Marryat, *Masterman Ready*

1. How many persons were on board the ship besides the captain?
2. Who do you think was the next person of importance above Masterman Ready in the ship?
3. Would you say that the age of Masterman Ready was over forty, over fifty, over sixty or over seventy?
4. Which word tells you that Masterman Ready was in good health?
5. The **taffrail** is a rail round part of the deck of the ship. Which word tells you whether the taffrail was at the front or at the back or in the middle of the ship?
6. What do you think was the cargo carried by the first ship on which Masterman Ready sailed?
7. What are the words used by the writer for **keep a ship on its proper course**?
8. How does the writer say **Masterman Ready nearly always knew what to do and how to do it**?
9. Which did the captain do most often: ask Masterman Ready what he thought or take his advice?
10. Did Masterman Ready run away to sea as a boy? Write down the words that tell you whether he did or not.

B. General
1. What name do we give to:
    (a) A straight line drawn across a circle through its centre?
    (b) A straight line drawn from one corner of a square to the opposite corner?
    (c) A straight line drawn from the centre of a circle to the circumference?
2. Write the following in full:
    I don't want c---rse oatmeal, of c---rse.
3. Which of the following words ought to have capital letters?
    the australian cricketers arrived on the queen mary.
4. Where'er you walk cool gales shall fan the glade.
    Write the word where'er in full.
5. Write out the following conversation using the correct punctuation:
    Im ready said Polly are you. Yes, Im ready said Jane
6. What do we call the homes of the following animals?
    (a) eagle (b) horse (c) pig.
7. There is a name for goods brought into a country by sea or air. What is it?
8. A three-sided figure drawn on paper is a . . . What?
    A **square**? A **rectangle**? A **triangle**? A **diagram**? or an **apex**?
9. I wish they would let you and . . . go with them. Which would you put in the blank—**me or I**?
10. Form a word from **tide** for the following sentence:
    The . . . waves near the mouth of the river are usually high.
11. Re-write, using only one word from each bracket:
    Have you (forgotten, forgot) how many lengths you have (swam, swim, swum)?
12. What is the opposite in meaning of:
    (a) **legible**   (b) **loyal?**
13. They said they thought he would keep his promise. What did they actually say?
14. Arrange the following in alphabetical order:
    John, Joseph, Jane, James, Jacob.
15. Which word in the brackets would best complete the following sentence?
    The Prime Minister's speech was followed by loud (apropos, appoints, applause, apathy).
16. "That's hitting below the belt!" I exclaimed. In other words, the person spoken of was—what?
    (a) Unfair? (b) Careless? (c) Hurting me? or (d) Boxing?
17. **Grendel was the monster's name. He lived in the marshes.**
    Make the above sentences into one sentence.
18. "Don't forget that you are responsible for our safety."
    Re-write the above sentence, beginning, "The responsibility . . .

TEST 17
A. Reading
THE COUNTRY MAID AND HER MILK PAIL

A country maid was on her way to market with a pail of milk on her head. As she walked along she began thinking, and this is what passed through her mind.

"I shall get enough money for the milk I am carrying to buy three hundred more eggs. I think I ought to get at least two hundred and fifty chicks from these eggs. The chicks will be ready to take to market just at the time when poultry are usually dear. This will mean that I shall be able to buy myself a new dress for Christmas. Now let me see—green would suit my complexion. Yes, it shall be a green dress. It will be rather nice to go to the fair in a new green dress. All the young men will notice me, but of course I shall take no notice of them."

As she thought of the young men and how she would toss her head in disdain as they passed by she could not help acting the part. She gave her head a toss and down came the pail. The milk was spilt and her wonderful dreams came to nothing.

It is this story we think of when we say, "Don't count your chickens before they are hatched."

ÆSOP

1. Which of these do you think was walking along to market:
   A little girl, a young woman or a middle-aged woman?
2. How many eggs did the maid expect would be of no use to her?
3. Two places are mentioned in the story where things are bought and sold. What are they?
4. Why did the maid decide to buy a **green** dress?
5. Would you say from the story that it was written at a time when eggs were cheap, dear or just about as dear as they are now? Why?
6. Would you say the maid was:
   (*a*) clever? (*b*) vain? (*c*) mean? or (*d*) handsome?
7. Which of the following would make the best title for the story?
   (*a*) **Not every egg produces a chick.**
   (*b*) **A stitch in time saves nine.**
   (*c*) **A bird in the hand is worth two in the bush.**
8. Find two words in the story which you could use instead of those in bold type in the following sentence.
   She looked at me **as though I was dirt.**
9. Think of the word **disdain** and then use it to make a word to say what kind of a toss the maid gave to her head.
10. A **maxim** is a rule of behaviour. What maxim does the story teach?

B. General

1. **If at first you don't suc—d try again.**
   Write the unfinished word in full.
2. What are the following **short** for?
   (*a*) Ave. (*b*) Gdns. (*c*) Rd. (*d*) Cres. (*e*) Sq.
3. Write the days of the week.
4. What are 'tis and 'twill short for?
5. Re-write, with quotation marks, and capitals only where necessary:
   MANY OF THE TEN COMMANDMENTS BEGIN WITH THOU SHALT NOT.
6. What name do we give to the homes of these creatures?
   (*a*) tiger (*b*) lion (*c*) fox.
7. The kind of animals that once lived but are no longer found anywhere to-day are said to be . . . What?
8. What do we call a person who collects and hoards money?
9. Re-write correctly:
   We mustn't stay no longer.
10. Form a word from **angel** for the following sentence:
    Dorothy had a most . . . disposition.
11. Form words from **bear** and **break** for the following sentence:
    I have . . . your carelessness a long time and now you have . . . another plate.
12. Change the word **pitiful** so that it has an opposite meaning.
13. "Is she glad?" I inquired.
    Re-write the above sentence beginning, I wanted to know . . .
14. What name can be given to the following:
    Pheasants, partridges, woodcock, grouse but not geese?
15. Which word in the brackets is best for finishing the following sentence?
    There are two kinds of pearls, one real the other (unreal, artificial, unlikely).
16. "They live from hand to mouth." In other words:
    (*a*) They do without knives and forks? (*b*) They eat nothing cooked?
    (*c*) They are hard up? or (*d*) They are savages?
17. Form one sentence from the following two, using the word **who.**
    The boy looked up the ladder. A man was coming down the ladder.
18. "Dr Brooks treated my father for asthma."
    Re-write the above sentence, beginning, "The treatment . . .

TEST 18
A. Reading
AN AFRICAN KING

The king, a good-looking, well-figured, tall young man of twenty-five, was sitting on a red blanket. The hair of his head was cut short, excepting on the top, where it was combed up into a high ridge, running from stem to stern like a cock's comb. On his neck was a very neat ornament—a large ring, of beautifully worked small beads, forming elegant patterns by their various colours. On one arm was another bead ornament, prettily devised; and on the other a wooden charm, tied by a string covered with snake-skin. On every finger and on every toe he had alternate brass and copper rings; and above the ankles, half-way up to the calf, a stocking of very pretty beads. Everything was light, neat, and elegant in its way; not a fault could be found with the taste of his "getting up." For a handkerchief he held a well-folded piece of bark, and a piece of gold-embroidered silk, which he constantly employed to hide his large mouth when laughing, or to wipe it after a drink of plantain-wine.

J. H. Speke, *Journal of the Discovery of the Source of the Nile*

1. Name a garment worn by the African king which is also worn in this country.

2. Name three parts of the body where this king wore rings.

3. Name three parts of the body where this king wore beads.

4. How many kinds of handkerchief did the king carry? What were they made of?

5. Find two words which mean **made in such a way as to look very nice**.

6. Which word does the writer use when he wants to say that something is **beautiful and nicely formed**? (One word only required.)

7. How does the writer say **from front to back**?

8. What did the king wear for its magic power?

9. Which word tells you that the brass and copper rings were arranged so that two of the same kind did not come together?

10. Find the words in the description for **he kept on using**.

B. General

1. **Write your name and ad——s in the space below.**
   What is the word that is unfinished above?
2. What words beginning with **t** and **r** rhyme with **muff**?
3. **Mary buys a paper called girls only.**
   Which words need capital letters in the above sentence?
4. Re-write and insert an apostrophe where needed.
   Tis seven oclock, I think.
5. Re-write the following in three lines with the necessary punctuation marks:
   Mary Mary quite contrary how does your garden grow.
6. Name the homes of the following:
   (*a*) gipsy (*b*) vicar (*c*) nun.
7. What is a person called when he is playing:
   (*a*) piano? (*b*) flute? (*c*) bag-pipes?
8. What name do we give to a person who is put to death because he will not give up his religion?
9. **It's no use me trying no more.**
   Which two words would you change to make the above sentence correct?
   What would you put in their place?
10. Form a word from **luxury** for the following sentence:
    The princess was used to a . . . style of living.
11. **Which horse have you . . . besides Topsy?**
    The word needed to complete the above sentence is formed from **ride**. What is it?
12. Add prefixes to make (*a*) **perfect** and (*b*) **own** opposite in meaning.
13. **"Why did you say that?" he asked me.**
    Re-write the above sentence beginning, **He asked me . . .**
14. What name have the following in common?
    Eye, nose, mouth, but not hand.
15. Which of the words in brackets is best for finishing the following sentence?
    Your presence at the ceremony is kindly (asked, requested, expected, called for).
16. **"What a wet blanket you are!"**
    This means that you are—what?
    (*a*) A spoil-sport? (*b*) A damp squib? (*c*) An umbrella maker?
    or (*d*) A "mac" minder?
17. Form a sentence from the two that follow using the word **which**:
    The book was entitled Oliver Twist. I lost it last week.
18. **"What Smith said about the accident was no doubt true."**
    Re-write the above sentence, beginning, **"The account . . .**

TEST 19
A. Reading
TABLE MANNERS AT THE ZOO

It was not long before the baby giant panda began to take some of her meals in public and have a tea-party of her own as the chimpanzees do. But first of all, the Zoo authorities thought it wise to hold a trial tea-party in private to see whether her table manners were good enough for public exhibition.

The trial was held in a corner of the Children's Zoo where a keeper had prepared for her a plate of sugar-cane, a jugful of bamboo shoots and a mugful of milk. Then the baby giant panda was allowed to "tuck in," the keeper standing beside her to see that she did not forget any of her table manners. She behaved so well that after another trial or two she was allowed to show herself in public during the same summer.

She learnt to drink her milk from the mug very quickly, just like the "tea-party" chimps, but her method of wielding the vessel was different from theirs because of her claws. A chimpanzee will grasp the mug by the handle and hold it up to his lips. The giant panda's method is to begin by scooping the mug towards her on the table; then, lowering her head, and gripping the rim in her teeth, she sits suddenly upright. The contents are thus neatly tilted down her throat. Only when the mug is empty does she grasp it with both her feet and holds it up while her tongue scours the inside for the very last drops.

[By kind permission of the *Evening Standard*.]

1. What are the people in charge of the Zoo called in the story?

2. **As the chimpanzees do.** Do **what**?

3. What are the people in charge of the animals called in the story?

4. Find a word in the story which may be used instead of **show**.

5. What prevents a baby panda from drinking her milk as a chimpanzee does?

6. How does the writer say **her way of using (or managing) a mug**?

7. Why does the baby giant panda sit suddenly upright during her meal?

8. Write down the word which tells you that the baby giant panda does not make a mess in drinking.

9. Can you find two words in the story beginning with **p** that are opposite in meaning?

10. How does the writer say **in this way**?

B. General

1. Our Queen is Elizabeth II. Long may she r---n!
   Write the missing word in full.
2. (*a*) **November 5th is Guy Fawkes' Day.**
   (*b*) **My birthday is on the 8th of March.**
   Write 5th and 8th as ordinary **words.**
3. The address on the letter was **44 high street, Bristol.**
   How would you have written this?
4. **He'd like to come but can't spare the time.**
   Write **he'd** and **can't** in full.
5. Re-write the following with the proper punctuation:
   Listen she said to what I have to say.
6. What are the creatures that live in these homes?
   (*a*) eyrie   (*b*) burrow   (*c*) pen **or** fold.
7. Write the name for the coat of wool on a sheep.
8. The air which covers the earth like a blanket is called . . . what?
9. Re-write the following sentence correctly:
   All the things what we seen were most interesting.
10. Form a word from **equal** for the following sentence:
    I believe in . . . of the sexes.
11. Re-write the following with a word formed from **tear**:
    So you have t— your clothes again!
12. Which word has a meaning opposite to that of **attach**?
13. **He put the question to her, would she go with him.**
    Re-write the sentence beginning, I said to her, ". . .
14. Arrange in alphabetical order:
    pull, push, pursue, punish, pulverise.
15. Which word in the brackets is best for completing the sentence below?
    This is a (true, valuable, genuine, strong) mink—yes, the real article.
16. "Sam was always at loggerheads with his schoolfellows." This means he was—what?
    (*a*) Peaceable?   (*b*) Amiable?   (*c*) Popular **or** (*d*) Quarrelsome?
17. Join the following sentences to make one by using the word **who.**
    The old man was feeling his way with a stick. He was blind.
18. "The game was spoiled by Dick losing his temper."
    Re-write the above sentence, beginning, "A loss of temper . . .

TEST 20
A. Reading
THE SHEPHERD'S WORK

The shepherd who takes charge of a large flock does little other work upon the farm, except to help at hay-making and harvest-time, for which he usually receives extra pay. His busiest and most anxious season is in the late winter and the early spring, when lambs are born; then not only will he be continually among his ewes by day, but will often spend night after night in a small wooden hut beside the fold. In it he lies down fully dressed, and wakens in an instant when he hears the feeble bleating of a new-born lamb. Lantern in hand, he goes out into the cold darkness of the night, sees that the little creature is doing well, can get upon its legs and suck.

When once the weather has become quite warm and settled comes the shearing of the sheep. The heavy fleeces would be most uncomfortable to them if they had to wear them all the summer; and, moreover, they are of great value to ourselves as wool. So, towards the end of May or early in the month of June, the shepherd has his shears well sharpened; and one morning, as you pass some barn or meadow, you will hear the steady sound of snipping as the fleece is swiftly cut away.

But just a day or two before the shearing-time the sheep are washed, so that the fleeces may be fairly clean when shorn. Each sheep is thrown into a pond or dammed-up stream, and while it swims and struggles to regain the bank, is rubbed with a long pole until the twelve months dirt accumulated in the muddy fields is scrubbed away.

A. O. Cooke, *Work and Workers* [by kind permission of Thomas Nelson & Sons, Ltd.]

1. What name do we give to a large number of sheep all together?
2. What do we call the coat of wool on a sheep's back?
3. How do we speak of the sheep when its wool has been cut off? We say that it has been—what?
4. What name is given to the mother sheep?
5. In which times of the year does the shepherd leave his sheep?
6. In which of the following months are lambs usually born—November, February, May or August?
7. What causes the "steady sound of snipping" that is spoken of in the extract?
8. Find a word in the extract for **collected together in a mass**.
9. Find a word for the field where the sheep are kept.
10. What do we call the sound made by a sheep when it cries?

B. General
1. **He was a cruel man and he made many en-m—s.**
   Write the unfinished word in full.
2. Write other words that have the **same sound** as:
   (*a*) nay   (*b*) slay   (*c*) way.
3. Here is a message in three sentences. Which words would you write with capital letters?
   can you come tomorrow father would like to see us you can stay for the week-end if you like.
4. **Ill meet you outside St Jamess Church**
   Write the above with proper punctuation.
5. Arrange the following in paragraphs correctly punctuated:
   What shall we need for the fire asked John sticks said Mary Paper said Alan Matches said Jane Good said John
6. What sort of people would you expect to find living in the following?
   (*a*) monastery   (*b*) log-cabin   (*c*) igloo.
7. Write the name for the skin of a cow.
8. Name the **tank** (or it may be **building**) in which fish are kept.
9. Re-write the following sentence correctly:
   I am the oldest of the twin brothers.
10. Form a word from **duty** for the following sentence:
    Sam had always been a . . . son.
11. Finish the sentence below with a word formed from **throw**.
    Here is a good loaf someone must have th---- away.
12. Change the words (*a*) **encourage** (*b*) **appear** so that they mean their opposites.
13. **"Where did you go yesterday?"**
    Re-write the above beginning, **I wonder where . . .**
14. What common name can you give to the following?
    Bin, bag, caddy, scuttle, box.
15. Which is the best word in brackets for completing the following sentence?
    Outside the bedroom on the first floor was a sunny (verandah, porch, gallery, balcony).
16. "You had better take the bull by the horns." This means, which?
    (*a*) Act and take a chance. (*b*) Hang on to what you have? **or** (*c*) Jump on to the bull's back?
17. Make one sentence from the three that follow.
    I like cakes. Mother makes cakes. I like Mother's cakes better than any others.
18. "The chairman said he would like some volunteers to come forward."
    Re-write the above sentence, beginning, "An appeal . . .

TEST 21
A. Reading
THE FOX AND THE CROW

It happened one day that a crow snatched a goodly piece of cheese out of an open shop window and flew off with it into a high tree, intent on enjoying the prize.

A fox spied the dainty morsel in the crow's beak and thought he would like it for himself. So he came up to the tree and said, "O Mistress Crow, how beautiful are your wings! how bright your eyes! how graceful your neck! Your breast is the breast of an eagle! Your claws—I beg your pardon, your talons—are a match for all the beasts of the field! What a pity it is that such a bird should be dumb, and miss perfection only in not having a voice!"

The crow, pleased with all this flattery, and chuckling to herself to think how she would surprise the fox with her caw, opened her mouth. Down dropped the cheese, and the fox at once snapped it up. As he walked away he was heard to observe that whatever he had said about the crow's beauty, he had said nothing about her brains.

ÆSOP

1. What was the **dainty morsel**?

2. Which word in the story could be a name for all that the fox said?

3. Which bird has **talons** instead of **claws**?

4. In what way did the fox say that the crow just missed being perfect?

5. How did the crow think she would show the fox that he was mistaken?

6. Why did the fox say what he did about the crow's voice?

7. Why did the fox say "I beg your pardon?"

8. Find a word in the story that means **say**.

9. Find a word in the story to describe a person unable to speak.

10. Find words in the story for the following:
    Thinking of nothing else but how nice it would be to feast on the cheese.

11. Why hadn't the fox said anything about the crow's brains?

12. What can we call the sentences that end with the sign (!)?

B. General

1. What words could you use instead of **nice** in
   (a) nice to **taste**; (b) nice to **smell**; (c) nice to **read**?
2. Write a word beginning with **an-** that means **old**.
3. **We are going to the channel islands for our holiday.**
   Do any of the above words need capital letters? If so, which?
4. **Id like to be a plumbers assistant.**
   Write **Id** and **plumbers** correctly.
5. Re-write the following with the proper punctuation:
   Come in said Mother and make yourself at home.
6. What would you write as the opposite of **superior**?
7. Write words beginning with **in-** which mean:
   (a) **not often**; (b) **not costing much.**
8. What do we call the flesh of young sheep when eaten?
9. Re-write the following correctly:
   Mary saw she could of killed him.
10. (a) Form a word from **picture** for the following sentence:
    It was a . . . scene.
    (b) Write another word that ends in the same manner.
11. Re-write the following sentence with words formed from **swear** and **take**:
    I could have . . . that you were the one who . . . it.
12. What word has a meaning opposite in meaning to:
    (a) **important**; (b) **exterior**?
13. **John inquired whether there was any room for him.**
    Re-write the above using the actual words John spoke.
14. What common name can you give to the following?
    Slippers, boots, shoes, sandals.
15. Which word in the brackets is best for completing the following sentence?
    Your son, sir, will grow up to be a (barber, barbarian, barbican, barbel) without manners.
16. The old man was hard of hearing means that he was—which?
    (a) Unwilling to listen? (b) Somewhat deaf?
    (c) A mumbling speaker? or (d) Inattentive?
17. Join up the following sentences to make one sentence, using the word **which**:
    The buses pass our door frequently. They go to Beyton and back.
18. "The boys were relieved when they were told they could go home."
    Re-write the above sentence, beginning, "Permission . . .

TEST 22
A. Reading
LONDON'S PRINCIPAL PLACES OF INTEREST

London, the capital of England, is the largest city in the world. Ships bringing cargoes and passengers from all over the world dock in the Thames, and Tower Bridge is opened several times a day to allow ships to pass. The City is the oldest part of London. Once a walled town, it occupies only 259 hectares of territory, but the most important business houses, the Bank of England, St Paul's Cathedral, the Tower of London and the Guildhall lie within its boundaries. In the city of Westminster are the Houses of Parliament, the Government Offices of Whitehall, the Prime Minister's residence in Downing Street, Westminster Abbey and the royal palaces.

The West End is the fashionable and modern district of London, the evening resort of theatregoers and diners. In the daytime Regent Street, Oxford Street and Piccadilly are thronged with shoppers, and only a few steps away in Soho, London's foreign quarter, are street markets for fruit, vegetables and even clothing.

A belt of parks and open spaces surrounds London's central business area—Kensington Gardens, Hyde Park, Green Park, St James's Park and Regent's Park. Near by is Buckingham Palace, the royal residence in London and centre of the State functions and pageantry of the city.

From *Films of Britain* [by kind permission of the British Travel and Holidays Association].

1. Where is London situated?

2. Name the four districts mentioned in London.

3. In which of these four districts does the Queen live?

4. Name a place in London in which you might expect to see Italians and Frenchman.

5. Name two streets in the West End of London.

6. In which district of London is Downing Street?

7. Would you say that the City of London occupies a large part of modern London, a fairly large part, a small part, or about half of it?

8. Which part of London mentioned is nearest the sea?

9. The City is the oldest part of London. Which is the most modern part mentioned?

10. What other city forms part of London?

B. General

1. Don't forget to si-- your name at the bottom of the paper.
   (a) Write the unfinished word in full.
   (b) Your name as you have written it is called your . . . what?
2. Write a word beginning with l that rhymes with **fatigue**.
3. If you were told to put two more capitals in the following, which words would you choose for them?
   Dickory dickory dock the mouse ran up the clock.
4. Wh— afraid of the big bad wolf?
   What should the first word in the above question be?
5. Re-write the following with correct punctuation:
   I never said I didnt said Alice you did said the Mock Turtle
6. Write in full the boys' names that are shortened to:
   (a) Pat (b) Dan (c) Ted.
7. What name do we give to the task of making a place strong against attack? We do **what** to it?
8. From what animals do we get the meat called:
   (a) veal (b) mutton (c) pork?
9. Re-write the following sentence correctly:
   It was me what broke the window.
10. Form a word from **circle** for the following sentences:
    (a) **The table was a . . . one.**
    (b) **The newspaper has a large . . .**
11. Was it you who . . . the bell just now?
    What is the missing word beginning with **r**?
12. Write the words that are opposite in meaning to:
    (a) **connect** (b) **do**.
13. **Anne said she would be going to London next day.**
    Write down what Anne actually said.
14. What is meant by the following?
    (a) O.H.M.S. (b) J.P. (c) U.S.A.
15. Which word in the brackets is best suited to the following sentence?
    A holiday at the seaside should (balance, batten, benefit, beach) the whole family.
16. "The children were all ears," means that they were—which?
    (a) Very large-eared? (b) Without other features?
    (c) Intent on listening? **or** (d) Dressed as ears of corn?
17. Make one sentence of the following, using the word **which**.
    This is my favourite desk. I do most of my writing at it.
18. "We should have liked Tom if he had not been so proud."
    Re-write the above sentence, beginning, "Tom's pride . . .

TEST 23
A. Reading
AN INDIAN CITY STREET

Not only are there always crowds of people in the streets of an Indian city but we see all kinds of animals which at home we could only see at a circus or in the Zoo.

Monkeys clamber over the roofs, and sneak down the sides of the houses to steal some fruit from the shops. Red and green parrots scream at one another, and in the middle of the street lies a white and brown hump-backed cow. No one would think of driving it away for it is sacred. If it lies down in the middle of the street that will bring good luck to the shopkeepers.

Then down the street comes a lordly elephant, with a brown man wearing a big turban sitting on its back. It moves along with huge strides and its trunk swings to and fro searching for some titbit.

A donkey plods along half hidden under a load of green, juicy leaves that are being taken to market. It stops for a moment while its owner chats to a friend. Red and brown chickens wander about the streets picking up morsels here and there.

Suddenly there is a shout. The owner of the donkey waves his stick, for a goat has been quietly nibbling away at the juicy green leaves on the donkey's back. His owner makes such a fuss that everyone stops to see what is the matter.

B. G. Hardingham, *Foundations of Geography* [by kind permission of Thomas Nelson & Sons, Ltd.]

1. How many kinds of four-footed animals are mentioned in the extract? Name them.

2. Which of these animals is looked upon as **holy**?

3. How many persons (besides the shopkeepers) are mentioned in the extract?

4. Which of them has no animal with him?

5. Which word tells you that the monkeys try not to be seen when they want to steal fruit?

6. Which of the men in the extract wears something on his head? What is it?

7. How does the writer say **backwards and forwards**?

8. Find two words in the extract which mean **very long steps**.

9. **Suddenly there is a shout.** Who shouts?

10. Find two words in the extract which can be used to describe small pieces of food.

B. General

1. What word containing the letter r and ending in --ten rhymes with **bitten and kitten?**
2. SHALL WE PLAY BLIND MAN'S BUFF.
   How would you write the above in your ordinary handwriting?
3. **Delicate; fragile; frail.**
   Which of these would you use in the following sentences?
   (a) The butterfly has . . . wings.
   (b) This wine glass is . . .
   (c) Elsie was a . . . lady.
4. I love little Pussy: . . . coat is so warm.
   Is the missing word **it's** or **its**?
5. Re-write the following sentences with proper punctuation:
   How do you know Im mad said Alice you must be said the Cat or you wouldn't come here.
6. What are the following girls' names short for?
   (a) Sue (b) Peggy (c) Vi (d) Di.
7. Find a name for food plants like **wheat, oats, barley** and **rice.**
8. Which animal gives us the meat called **venison?**
9. Re-write the following sentence as it should be written:
   Him and me went up to the top of the hill.
10. Form a word from **study** to complete the following sentence:
    The . . . young man became a great scholar.
11. Re-write the following in the past tense:
    I run after the thief and catch him at the station.
12. Form from (a) **visible** and (b) **courteous** words with opposite meanings.
13. **The sailor said that his ship would remain in the bay.**
    Write what you think the sailor actually said.
14. What common name can be given to the following?
    Milk, water, ink, petrol.
15. Which word in the brackets is best for completing the following sentence?
    We walked round the lake picking the daffodils growing wild on the (margin, marine, marline, maroon).
16. "To make a clean breast of it," means—what?
    (a) To wash thoroughly? (b) To pluck the feathers well?
    (c) To tell everything? or (d) To clean one's chest?
17. Make one sentence of the following using **who, whom** or **which.**
    Mary is a good friend. I spend many happy hours with her.
18. "We could not see their faces because of the headlights."
    Re-write the above, beginning, "The glare . . .

TEST 24
A. Reading
WINDSOR CASTLE

Windsor Castle, on a chalk cliff rising abruptly above the Thames, has been for 850 years the chief residence of the Sovereigns of England. It was built by William the Conqueror, and extended by Henry III and Edward III. Edward III was born here in 1312, and Henry VI in 1421, and three kings (David of Scotland, John of France, and James I of Scotland) have been imprisoned within its walls. The present appearance of the building dates from extensive restorations undertaken by Wyatville under George IV.

On entering the Lower Ward from Castle Hill by Henry VIII's Gateway we have, on our right, the houses of the Military Knights of Windsor (an order founded by Edward III). Straight ahead are the Horseshoe Cloisters (1474–83) and the Curfew Tower with its 13th century dungeon.

From the Blue Guide to England, *Muirhead's England* [by kind permission of Ernest Benn, Ltd.]

1. How long ago did a king first live in Windsor Castle?

2. Name the river that flows by at the foot of the castle.

3. Which word tells you that the chalk cliff is **steep**?

4. Windsor Castle is the chief residence of the sovereign. Name another royal residence in England.

5. How many kings are named in the above passage?

6. Which word is used for **repairs** in the passage?

7. What name do we give to a person who does the kind of work that Wyatville did?

8. Find a word in the passage for a sheltered or covered walk.

9. In which century were the Horseshoe Cloisters built?

10. What would you expect to find in a "Curfew Tower"?

11. What is beneath the Curfew Tower?

12. Write the name of our present sovereign.

B. General

1. No one likes to sit in a cold and dra---ty classroom.
   Write the unfinished word in full.
2. What word beginning with z (the name of a metal) rhymes with **ink**?
3. LITTLE BOY BLUE COME BLOW ME YOUR HORN.
   Re-write the above sentence with three capital letters only.
4. What is **won't** short for in:
   Won't you play with us?
5. Re-write the following with proper punctuation:
   Hold your tongue said the Queen turning purple I wont said Alice Off with her head the Queen shouted at the top of her voice.
6. What are the following boys' names short for?
   (*a*) Jim   (*b*) Sam   (*c*) Bob.
7. Hard materials like metals are sometimes given a coloured glass-like coating. What is this coating called?
8. What do we call (*a*) a **tin** (*b*) a **wooden case**—in which tea is kept?
9. Re-write correctly:
   These shoes have wore out quick.
10. Form a word from **rich** for the following sentence:
    The king did much to . . . the nation.
11. Write out the following with one word only from each bracket:
    I wish I had (knew, known, knowed) before (who, which, what) was (hid, hided, hidden) in the box.
12. Form words from (*a*) **useful** and (*b*) **place** that have opposite meanings.
13. **Father said that he was glad to see me.**
    Write down Father's actual words.
14. What book is it that will tell you the **position** of a town or mountain in any country?
15. Which word in the brackets is best for finishing this sentence?
    The attackers made a (breach, breech, broach, brooch) in the castle wall.
16. "She led them up the garden path very nicely," means that she:
    (*a*) Entertained them? (*b*) Took them through to the house?
    (*c*) Deceived them? or (*d*) Saw them to the gate?
17. Make a single sentence from the following two, using the word **who**.
    A man knocked at our door. He was looking for his wife.
18. "The visitors will leave tomorrow at noon."
    Re-write the above sentence, beginning, "The departure . . .

TEST 25
A. Reading
THE TRAVELLERS AND THE BEAR

One day, two friends who were travelling along the same road together met with a bear. One of them was seized with fright and without a thought for his companion climbed up into a tree and hid himself in the branches.

The other one saw at once that he would not be able to get the better of the bear by himself, and as he had no time to escape he threw himself on the ground and pretended to be dead. He did this because he had been told that a bear would never touch a dead body.

As he lay there he heard the bear approach him. In a few moments the creature began to snuff about his nose and ears and heart. The man held himself quite still without breathing, and at last the bear, to his great relief, took him to be dead, and walked away.

As soon as the bear was well out of sight the man who had hidden himself in the tree came down. He ran up to his friend in high spirits. He began to make jokes about their escape. "What was it the bear whispered to you?" he asked, "for I noticed that the beast put his mouth very close to your ear."

"Why," replied his friend, "it was no great secret. He advised me to be careful about the sort of company I kept, and in particular, to avoid those who leave their friends in the lurch when they themselves get into difficulty."

ÆSOP

1. What other two words are used in the story instead of **bear**?
2. Why did one of the men climb up into a tree without thinking of his friend?
3. Why did one of the men throw himself on the ground and pretend to be dead?
4. Why didn't the bear touch the man on the ground?
5. The man on the ground did two things to make the bear think he was dead. What were they?
6. What word is used instead of **friend** in the story?
7. What is said in the story which means the opposite to **stick to their friends**?
8. Why did the man in the tree come down in high spirits?
9. What did the man who came down from the tree pretend?
10. Why did the man on the ground say what he did at the end of the story? Choose the right answer below and write (*a*), (*b*) or (*c*).
    - (*a*) Because it was what the bear said to him.
    - (*b*) Because he thought it would please his friend.
    - (*c*) Because he felt annoyed with his friend.

L. General
1. Write the name of the first, second and eighth month in the year.
2. Write a word ending in -es that rhymes with **buzz**.
3. LITTLE JACK HORNER SAT IN A CORNER EATING HIS CHRISTMAS PIE.
    Re-write the above as three lines of verse and with six capital letters only.
4. When I saw her last she was entering the (lady's, ladies, ladies', ladys') **enclosure.**
    Which of the words in brackets is correct?
5. How many sweets asked Tom shall I get for 5p Oh six or seven said the shopkeeper then I'll have seven said Tom
    Re-write the above conversation with proper stops and quotation marks.
6. Write in full the boys' names that correspond to:
    (*a*) Sandy (*b*) Dick (*c*) Tom.
7. What do we call the edge of a piece of cloth which is so finished off that the threads will not become loose?
8. What instrument enables you to see a very tiny object by making it larger and more distinct?
9. Re-write the following sentence with **swum** and **swam** used correctly:
    We . . . all afternoon as we had . . . all afternoon the day before.
10. Form a word from **weary** for the following sentence:
    The tired children trudged . . . home.
11. Re-write with suitable words in the blanks:
    Neither you . . . he can go. Both of you . . . too ill.
12. The referee **allowed** the goal. What word opposite in meaning can be formed from **allow**?
13. **Margaret said that she hadn't seen me for a long time.**
    Write what you think Margaret actually said.
14. In what book would you look for the address of a shopkeeper?
15. Which word in the brackets is best for finishing the sentence below?
    I saw him on the bridge leaning on the (parquet, parapet, paradox, paramount).
16. "Our M.P. likes to sit on the fence." This means that he:
    (*a*) Likes the country? (*b*) Likes a gossip?
    (*c*) Dislikes taking sides? **or** (*d*) Likes balancing exercises?
17. Make a single sentence of the following:
    Jones passed the ball to Smith. Smith was waiting on the right wing. Jones received the ball from Brown.
18. "The committee made up their minds to resign."
    Re-write the above sentence, beginning, "The decision . . .

TEST 26
A. Reading
SURNAMES

Family names did not come into use in this country for some centuries after the Norman Conquest.

Our ancestors lived in very small villages or hamlets where everybody knew who John or Stephen or Hugh was. It was not until the hamlets grew and men began to travel that the need arose for a second distinguishing name.

Surnames—really "sire-names" or names of fathers—then began to come into use, and John began to be distinguished from all other Johns by being John, son of, say Reynold, or as we now call his remote descendant, Reynoldson, or Reynolds.

Johnson and Stephenson are the same kind of name.

Then there were trades which helped to distinguish one John from another. There was John the Baker, John the Miller, John the Tailor, and so on. It is easy to understand that this would give us John Baker, John Miller and John Tailor. Perhaps you will remember Wat Tyler in your history book. He was Walter the Tiler.

Place names are also common. There were perhaps two Stephens in a village. One lived on the hill, the other on the moor. So one became Stephen of the hill, or Stephen Hill, and the other Stephen of the moor, or Stephen Moore.

To one of these sources—father's name, trade, dwelling-place—practically all our surnames are traceable.

1. Give another name for **family names**.

2. What are hamlets?

3. Family names may be traced to three sources. What are they?

4. What is meant by **a sire**?

5. Why was it that surnames were once unnecessary?

6. Which of the following dates saw the beginning of the Norman Conquest: 55 B.C.? A.D. 500? A.D. 1066? **or** A.D. 1588?

7. What do we call the people of our race or family who lived long ago?

8. How many Christian names are mentioned in the extract? Write them down.

9. How many trades are mentioned in the extract? Write them down.

10. How does the writer say "nearly all?"

B. General
1. Write two words ending in -iage that rhyme.
2. What are the words used to name smaller creatures of the same kind as:
    (a) sheep (b) swans (c) eagles (d) geese?
3. LITTLE MISS MUFFETT SAT ON A TUFFET EATING HER CURDS AND WHEY.
    Re-write the above as three lines of verse and with five capital letters only.
4. **We gave away toms old shoes but kept marys old hats.**
    Re-write correctly the words that have mistakes in them.
5. Re-write the following with proper punctuation:
    Now Sam said Mr Pickwick the first thing to be done is to order dinner Sir interposed Sam.
6. What are the **full** names corresponding to:
    (a) Liz (b) Joe (c) Flo (d) Pam?
7. A person who gives up his work and takes a long journey to visit a holy place is called a . . . what?
8. What instrument enables you to see plainly an object which is a very long way off?
9. Re-write with **rung** or **rang** in the blanks:
    We have . . . the bells today but the others . . . them yesterday.
10. Form a word from **friend** for the following sentence:
    I shall remember how you have . . . me.
11. Re-write the following with one word only from each bracket:
    The man asked me the name of the girl (who, which, what) had (come, came) with me.
12. All men are **mortal**. What word is opposite in meaning to **mortal**?
13. **I have lost my mother said the little boy.**
    Re-write the above beginning, The little boy said that . . .
14. What do you call the kind of book in which you keep photographs?
15. Which word in the brackets would best complete the following sentence?
    The tramps avoided the main roads and kept to the lanes and (highways, byways, thoroughfares, promenades).
16. "I hear that you are in the master's black books" means—what?
    (a) On his register? (b) Qualified for a prize?
    (c) Named as next monitor? or (d) In trouble with him?
17. Make a single sentence of the following:
    The dog chased the cat. The dog saw the cat in the garden.
18. "The skater was graceful and elegant in all she did so that the spectators were thrilled."
    Re-write the above, beginning, "The grace . . .

TEST 27
A. Reading
BLAZING THE TRAIL

Just as the sun rose they turned into the coconut grove, and were soon out of sight of the tents.

"Now, Master William, do you know," said Ready, stopping after they had walked twenty metres, "by what means we may find our way back again; for you see this forest of trees is rather puzzling, and there is no path to guide us?"

"No, I am sure I cannot tell; I was thinking of the same thing when you spoke; and of Tom Thumb who strewed peas to find his way back, but could not do it because the birds picked them all up."

"Well, Tom Thumb did not manage well, and we must try to do better; we must do as the Americans always do in their woods—we must *blaze* the trees."

"*Blaze* them! what, set fire to them?" replied William.

"No, no, Master William. *Blaze* is a term they use when they cut a slice of the bark off the trunk of a tree with one blow of a sharp axe, as a mark to find their way back again. They do not blaze every tree, but about every tenth tree as they go along, first one to the right, and then one to the left, which is quite sufficient; and it is very little trouble—they do it as they walk along, without stopping. So now we'll begin; you take the other side, it will be more handy for you to have your hatchet in your right hand; I can use my left. See now—just slice off the bark—the weight of the axe does it almost, and it will serve as a guide through the forest for years."

"What an excellent plan," observed William, as they walked along, occasionally marking the trees.

Captain Marryat, *Masterman Ready*

1. Which of the following means the same as **blazing the trail**?
   Firing the trees—Marking the path—Showing the light—Following the scent.
2. Which word tells you that one of the speakers is a boy?
3. Find a word in the passage which means **now and again**.
4. What did William think **blaze** meant?
5. About how many trees did each of the two blaze in every hundred passed?
6. Tom Thumb "could not do it." **Do** what?
7. Find **two** names given to the tool used to blaze the trees.
8. Name something, spoken of, that was not in the forest.
9. What is mentioned that tells you that the travellers were in a hot country?
10. What is the forest called by the writer besides a forest?

B. General

1. **Pay this bill for me and ask for a rec—t.**
   Write the unfinished word in full.
2. What word describes the following actions?
   (*a*) Taking the bones out of a fish.
   (*b*) Disinfecting a room by gas to get rid of germs or of insects.
3. Re-write the following with three capital letters only.
   MY FAVOURITE ENGLISH KING IS ALFRED.
4. **Id like to see the womens hospital.**
   Re-write Id and womens correctly.
5. Copy the following sentences and insert the necessary punctuation.
   Stop said Mr Pickwick What now said Wardle
6. What feminine names correspond to:
   (*a*) stallion and colt; (*b*) bull and bullock?
7. Handwriting and printing in which the letters stand out clearly and so are easily read is said to be . . . what?
8. From which trees do we get (*a*) acorns, (*b*) dates, (*c*) conkers?
9. We . . . lemonade at the party this year though previously it was orangeade that we had . . .
   Re-write the above using drank or drunk for the blanks.
10. Form a word from grass for the following sentence:
    The sheep were left to . . . in the meadow.
11. What name do we give to a number of people lined up to enter a shop or a cinema?
12. When an argument is the opposite of logical we say it is . . . what?
13. **I told him that I would never send him away.**
    Write down the words actually spoken by me.
14. What do you call the subject which you study in order to know about the stars and other heavenly bodies?
15. Which word in the brackets is best for finishing the following sentence?
    The way was dangerous and the men advanced with great (cause, caution, cavalry, causality).
16. To take a person down a peg means to do—what?
    (*a*) Take a peg from him? (*b*) Take down his coat for him?
    (*c*) Give him a drink? **or** (*d*) Give him reason for thinking less well of himself?
17. Make the following two sentences into one using the word whom.
    This is Tom Burns. I go fishing with him sometimes.
18. "I don't think you have much chance of winning."
    Re-write the above, beginning, "The chance . . .

ANSWERS

TEST 1
A

1. Bible. 2. goat. 3. three. 4. by shooting with bow and arrow. 5. the chase. 6. I am obliged to repair them. 7. read. 8. He had a wife. 9. The fire goes out. 10. By rubbing sticks together. 11. fatigued. 12. food and clothing.

B

1. potatoes. 2. fourth, twelfth. 3. It's a long way to Tipperary. 4. Apple, pears, bananas, grapes and oranges. 5. "I'm ready, sir," she said. 6. She was the Queen's daughter. 7. (a) grocer; (b) chemist. 8. allow. 9. Between you and me. 10. Alan was a lad of great strength. 11. Bite a piece off . . . bitten. 12. (a) disagreeable; (b) sense. 13. Tom said that he was coming. 14. canary, cement, cherub, chief, child. 15. microphone. 16. not very well. 17. This is the house that Jack built. 18. His strength was like a lion's (*or* that of a lion).

TEST 2
A

1. three. 2. mare. 3. foal. 4. A picture in a comic paper. 5. graze. 6. inquisitive. 7. terrified. 8. evening. 9. investigate. 10. apparently. 11. stallion. 12. neighing.

B

1. truly. 2. (a) century; (b) twentieth. 3. You may bring Mary when you come to see us on Monday. 4. semi-colon. 5. "Go away at once!" she exclaimed. 6. I spoke to the lady's maidservant. 7. (a) jeweller; (b) cutler. 8. fellow-worker. 9. did. 10. miraculous. 11. drunk. 12. show your ignorance. 13. He said that he would go but he didn't mean it. 14. arrival, baker, break, butcher, centre. 15. plumb-line. 16. (*b*). 17. The man held up his hand for a bus that was passing to stop. 18. The space left between the lines must be two centimetres.

TEST 3
A

1. saw, hatchet, powder, shot, gun. 2. semi-colon. 3. "most barbarous shape." 4. sun, rain. 5. thong. 6. goat. 7. goat-skin. 8. knees. 9. It was not really short. 10. boots *or* leggings.

B

1. pianos. 2. geography. 3. Robert Louis Stevenson is the author of Treasure Island. 4. It is a nice cake. Do you not think so? 5. "Do you really think so?" John said. 6. The duke was accompanied by his son. 7. chauffeur. 8. attack. 9. any. 10. wisdom. 11. eaten. 12. immodest. 13. Jack asked if he might leave early. 14. smack, small, smear, smock, smoke. 15. stethoscope. 16. In low spirits. 17. Mr. Jones invited inside the strange man who appeared at the door. 18. His rise to power took place (occurred) in the thirteenth century.

TEST 4
A

1. windmill, watermill. 2. vat. 3. softwood trees. 4. Russia, Canada. 5. rags, esparto grass. 6. cough. 7. Spain. 8. "Really!" I exclaimed. 9. Three—cutting down trees, sawing into logs, grinding into pulp. 10. In talking of fruit-pulp. 11. Seven. 12. oak, walnut, mahogany.

B
1. their. 2. ninth. 3. (a) stationary; (b) stationer's. 4. It's a fine day for the swallow and its young. 5. Peter said to the policeman, "Will you tell me the time, please?" 6. How can a spinster be a widow? 7. cannibals. 8. sent away. 9. My mother taught me to read. 10. popularity. 11. flown. 12. (a) misbehave; (b) disbelieve. 13. Mary asked Tom to help her to carry her box. 14. i a a e o u. 15. barometer. 16. (b). 17. although. 18. The speech of the Mayor lasted (occupied, took, etc.) forty minutes.

TEST 5
A
1. lair. 2. (little) creature. 3. "besought him... offended." 4. rope. 5. one who had previously saved his life. 6. "without more ado." 7. insignificant. 8. lion's. 9. the lion. 10. prey. 11. tone. 12. favour.

B
1. tongue. 2. Dutch. 3. Cyprus is an island in the Mediterranean. 4. I've come to see you, sir. 5. "Oh, what fun!" we all exclaimed. 6. My sister has four doe rabbits. 7. transparent. 8. torment. 9. lay, its. 10. (a) quarrelsome; (b) quarrelling. 11. drawn. 12. By *im*—impolite. 13. The little girl said that she had been naughty. 14. (a) cash on delivery; (b) Member of Parliament. 15. capacity. 16. boasting. 17. whether. 18. No explanation of your absence is necessary (needed, required).

TEST 6
A
1. poultry. 2. April, May. 3. bran, barley meal, oil. 4. hen. 5. cock. 6. grubs, worms. 7. cockerel. 8. strut. 9. cock. 10. cock, hen, cockerel, chick. 11. morsel. 12. principal.

B
1. knives, dessert, laid. 2. Saturday. 3. Tiger Hunting. 4. (a) girl's; (b) girls'. 5. "Tell me, madam. Is this the way to the Town Hall?" I said. 6. Will you let your uncle know that his nephew is here? 7. matron. 8. curious. 9. anything, any. 10. generosity. 11. risen. 12. (a) irregular; (b) valueless (*not* invaluable). 13. John asked Edna if she knew where his mother had gone. 14. omnibus, perambulator, telephone, promenade. 15. maltreated. 16. He ran away. 17. lest. 18. There is no need for you to come unless you like.

TEST 7
A
1. The half with the jam. 2. As in No. 1. 3. she peeped. 4. for fair play. 5. shall not. 6. the best piece. 7. "A bitter tone." 8. Shut her eyes. 9. "Ha-a-a!" 10. Maggie.

B
1. believed, received, besieged, seized. 2. centenary. 3. I went to the Regal Cinema to see "Richard the Third." 4. children's. 5. "Indeed," he said. "Do you know who I am?" 6. His brother has become a monk. 7. a bully. 8. spectators. 9. seen, went. 10. gift. 11. Practice makes perfect; therefore, practise. 12. disorder. 13. Sarah said that Ben thought he could do as he liked. 14. 10th day of this month. 15. mishap. 16. (c). 17. Henry was late for school through losing his satchel. 18. The explosion of the mine was seen by thousands.

TEST 8
A

1. To make the lions move about. 2. three. 3. den. 4. various attitudes. 5. astonishment, fear. 6. lashing his tail, snarling, showing his fangs. 7. about three years. 8. He kept at a "respectable distance." 9. "Quite indifferent apparently to the people outside." 10. The lion "appeared not to notice" him.

B

1. waist. 2. science. 3. (a) Louis the Fourteenth; (b) Henry the Fifth. 4. All is. 5. "I wish Mary would come soon," sighed her mother. 6. The wizard cast his spell on the prince. 7. oasis. 8. audience. 9. too, had risen. 10. depth. 11. In vain we tried to stop the blood from her cut vein. 12. disconnect. 13. Nan asked her father if she might go with him. 14. mint, tannery, foundry. 15. accompaniment. 16. (d). 17. Jane has a dog (of) which she is very fond (of). 18. The celebration of our victory will take place (be held) tomorrow.

TEST 9
A

1. Alice. 2. curious. 3. He was afraid the Duchess might hear. 4. Where is; it is. 5. Because one queen only was meant. 6. "She's under sentence of execution." 7. Duke. 8. anxiety. 9. timidity. 10. the Duchess boxed the Queen's ears. 11. tiptoe. 12. Where the Duchess was.

B

1. guess, concealed. 2. liquids. 3. Do you sell French wine or Danish butter? 4. shall not, will not. 5. "Beware!" I shouted. "There's a lion about!" 6. (a) cub; (b) gosling; (c) puppy. 7. pupils. 8. (a) congregation; (b) mob. 9. which. 10. energetic. 11. No sooner had she begun to row than the boat sank. 12. (a) unscrew; (b) misjudge. 13. Philip said to Susan that he hated her. 14 (a) byre; (b) hangar; (c) library. 15. accused. 16. (d). 17. The animal that belongs to the man next door howls all night. 18. A wise choice is needed (required, necessary) if you are going to win.

TEST 10
A

1. "Now for a frolic." 2. gale. 3. squall. 4. apples and oranges. 5. by fastening them with kerchiefs. 6. shop signs. 7. poultry. 8. (a) trundling; (b) whisking. 9. (a) gobbled; (b) screamed. 10. free from mishaps.

B

1. weighing, heavier, I. 2. cough. 3. in. 4. You will have to tell all that has occurred. 5. "Ah!" she cried. "There you are at last!" 6. (a) eaglet; (b) leveret; (c) foal. 7. surgeon. 8. every year. 9. whose, taken. 10. pride. 11. any. 12. illegal, uninterested (*not* dis-). 13. Steve said that he had seen (me) the previous day. 14. (a) tea; (b) sword; (c) clothes; (d) coal. 15. addict. 16. (*a*). 17. They discovered a cave which led them deep into the cliff. 18. A collision between the two cars seemed unavoidable (inevitable).

TEST 11
A

1. two. 2. semi-colon. 3. The gate was too high. 4. The road was long and straight. 5. To get away from the gate. 6. thorns. 7. the reins. 8. you. 9. He wanted to teach him a lesson. 10. the boy. 11. Where's the boy? *or* What has happened to the boy? 12. that remark.

B

1. muscles. 2. proceeded, preceded. 3. Saturday, London. 4. cannot, you are. 5. "If it's hot," mother said, "you can take your coat off." 6. (a) tadpoles; (b) nestlings; (c) elvers. 7. observatory. 8. (c). 9. you and me. 10. various. 11. given, rang. 12. rustless. 13. Will said that he hadn't seen (us) lately. 14. (a) asinine; (b) canine; (c) feline. 15. adhesive. 16. (d). 17. Father, who wore a green linen shirt, walked on our right. 18. A change of job between the men was suggested by the manager.

TEST 12
A

1. Jamaica. 2. three metres. 3. one hundred and fifty. 4. one and a half metres. 5. three. 6. They are green, not yellow. 7. cutlass. 8. one. 9. huge and giant. 10. on the flower-spike. 11. cluster. 12. They grow upwards not downwards.

B

1. language. 2. 55 years before the birth of Christ. 3. A Day on a Desert Island. 4. I'm sure they're right. 5. All I could say was, "Good gracious!" 6. (a) grubs; (b) caterpillars; (c) tadpoles. 7. vague, Plague. 8. physician. 9. may. 10. strengthening. 11. stolen, taken. 12. ignoble. 13. John said, "Don't make yourself . . . of it." 14. lion-like, horse-like, cow-like, sheep-like. 15. adequate. 16. (b). 17. I offered some old shoes to the (barefooted) beggar (who was barefooted). 18. Our order was that the boys must (should) finish their work before midnight.

TEST 13
A

1. lion, zebra, elephant, gorilla. 2. the lion. 3. "semi-somnolent condition." 4. "By an involuntary impulse." 5. majestic. 6. inevitably. 7. "The roar was uttered." 8. "My heart quailed within me." 9. "I beheld a sight." 10. his fear.

B

1. definite. 2. His Royal Highness. 3. Go, Tom, Tell. 4. Where there's a will there's a way. 5. "Open your mouth," said the doctor. "Now keep quite still." 6. (a) ram, ewe; (b) drake, duck. 7. admiral. 8. comfort. 9. taller. 10. heroism. 11. beaten. 12. displeasure. 13. "The manager will soon be back." 14. dwellings (homes, habitations). 15. admitted. 16. (b). 17. The wounded soldier tried to stand up to salute the general who passed by without seeing him. 18. The nobility of his appearance (person) struck us all.

TEST 14
A

1. To be able to get away, if necessary. 2. an Inn (or public house). 3. It was the name of the inn. 4. oaths. 5. the stranger. 6. Black Dog. 7. Black Dog. 8. fugitive. 9. chine. 10. the signboard of the Inn.

B

1. scissors. 2. dough. 3. (a). 4. 'Twas in Trafalgar Bay. 5. "Say 'Ninety-nine'." That was what the doctor said. 6. (a) cock, hen; (b) cob, pen. 7. Fall. 8. careless. 9. lying. 10. magical. 11. hidden. 12. abnormal. 13. "I think I shall be able to go." 14. bulbs. 15. agreeable. 16. (d). 17. The troops came to a beautiful mansion that was standing empty and desolate. 18. The organization of the party was undertaken by the secretary.

TEST 15
A
1. Elephants at Play. 2. "Making no noise." 3. "Almost casually." 4. bog, swamp. 5. bamboos, cedars. 6. elephants, tick-birds, ticks. 7. "Two elderly elephants sparred playfully." 8. with its trunk. 9. several trees, "a clump of cedars." 10. a cow elephant.

B
1. (a) guaranteed; (b) handkerchief. 2. (a) less; (b) fewer. 3. The largest city in the British Isles is London. 4. soldiers'. 5. three. "Good!" said John. / "Rotten!" said Tom. / "O.K." said Harry. 6. The heir to the throne is his nephew. 7. exports. 8. kind-hearted. 9. hurt, broken. 10. troublesome. 11. piece, peace. 12. merciless (un-). 13. I asked him whether he thought I should be better soon. 14. metals. 15. apertures. 16. (c). 17. She returned hurriedly to the cottage (in) which she lived (in). 18. The splendour of the wedding was admitted by everyone (all).

TEST 16
A
1. four. 2. first mate. 3. over sixty. 4. hale. 5. aft. 6. coal. 7. navigate a vessel. 8. "He was seldom at a loss." 9. ask his opinion. 10. No—"having been bound apprentice."

B
1. (a) diameter; (b) diagonal; (c) radius. 2. I don't want coarse oatmeal, of course. 3. The Australian, Queen Mary. 4. wherever. 5. "I'm ready," said Polly. "Are you?" / "Yes, I'm ready," said Jane. 6. (a) eyrie; (b) stable; (c) sty. 7. imports. 8. triangle. 9. me. 10. tidal. 11. Have you forgotten how many lengths you have swum? 12. (a) illegible; (b) disloyal. 13. "We think he will keep his promise." 14. Jacob, James, Jane, John, Joseph. 15. applause. 16. (a). 17. Grendel was the name of the monster that lived in the marshes. (The name of the monster that lived in the marshes was Grendel.) 18. The responsibility for our safety, don't forget, is yours (rests on you).

TEST 17
A
1. A young woman. 2. fifty. 3. market, fair. 4. to suit her complexion. 5. cheap—because she could get so many eggs for one pail of milk. 6. vain. 7. (c). 8. "In disdain." 9. disdainful. 10. "Don't count your chickens before they are hatched."

B
1. succeed. 2. (a) Avenue; (b) gardens; (c) road; (d) crescent; (e) square. 3. Sunday, Monday, etc. 4. It is *and* it will. 5. Many of the ten commandments begin with "Thou Shalt Not." 6. (a) lair; (b) den; (c) earth. 7. extinct (prehistoric). 8. miser. 9. We musn't stay any longer. 10. angelic. 11. borne, broken. 12. pitiless. 13. . . . if she was glad. 14. game. 15. artificial. 16. (c). 17. The boy looked up the ladder at a man who was coming down. 18. The treatment of my father for asthma was carried out (done) by Dr Brooks.

TEST 18
A
1. a stocking. 2. neck, finger, toe. 3. neck, arm, legs. 4. Two—bark and silk. 5. "prettily devised." 6. elegant. 7. "from stem to stern." 8. a wooden charm. 6. alternate. 10. "constantly employed."

B
1. address. **2.** tough, rough. **3.** Girls Only. **4.** " 'Tis seven o'clock," I think.
5. Mary, Mary, / Quite contrary, / How does your garden grow? **6.** (a) caravan;
(b) vicarage; (c) convent. **7.** (a) pianist; (b) flautist; (c) piper. **8.** martyr. **9.** *my*
for *me* and *any* for *no*. **10.** luxurious. **11.** ridden. **12.** imperfect, disown. **13.** He
asked me why I had said that. **14.** They are features. **15.** requested. **16.** (*a*).
17. The book which I lost last week was entitled Oliver Twist. **18.** The account
of the accident that (which) Smith gave was no doubt true.

TEST 19
A
1. "The Zoo authorities." **2.** have a tea-party. **3.** keepers. **4.** exhibition. **5.** her
claws. **6.** "her method of wielding the vessel." **7.** to tilt the milk into her mouth.
8. neatly. **9.** public, private. **10.** thus.
B
1. reign. **2.** fifth, eighth. **3.** 44 High Street, Bristol. **4.** He would, cannot.
5. "Listen," she said, "to what I have to say." **6.** (a) eagle; (b) rabbit; (c) sheep.
7. fleece. **8.** atmosphere. **9.** All the things that (which) we saw were most interesting. **10.** equality. **11.** torn. **12.** detach. **13.** I said to her, "Will you come with
me?" **14.** pull, pulverise, punish, pursue, push. **15.** genuine. **16.** (*d*). **17.** The old
man who was blind was feeling his way with a stick. **18.** A loss of temper by Dick
(on Dick's part) spoilt the game.

TEST 20
A
1. A flock. **2.** a fleece. **3.** shorn. **4.** ewe. **5.** at haymaking and harvesting.
6. February. **7.** the shears. **8.** accumulated. **9.** fold. **10.** bleating.
B
1. enemies. **2.** (a) neigh; (b) sleigh; (c) weigh. **3.** Can, Father, You. **4.** I'll
meet you outside St James's Church. **4.** "What shall we need for the fire?" asked
John. / "Sticks," said Mary. / "Paper," said Alan. / "Matches," said Jane. / "Good,"
said John. **6.** (a) monks; (b) lumberjacks; (c) Eskimos. **7.** hide. **8.** aquarium.
9. I am the elder of the twin brothers. **10.** dutiful. **11.** thrown. **12.** (a) discourage;
(b) disappear. **13.** I wonder where you went yesterday. **14.** receptacles (containers).
15. balcony. **16.** (*a*). **17.** I like the cakes which mother makes better than any
others. **18.** An appeal for volunteers to come forward was made by the chairman.

TEST 21
A
1. a piece of cheese. **2.** flattery. **3.** eagle. **4.** in not having a voice. **5.** by opening
her mouth to sing. **6.** to make her speak. **7.** he had made a slip in saying "claws."
8. observe. **9.** dumb. **10.** "Intent on enjoying the prize." **11.** He thought nothing
of them. **12.** Exclamations.
B
1. (a) delicious; (b) fragrant; (c) interesting. **2.** ancient (antique). **3.** Channel
Islands. **4.** I should, plumber's. **5.** "Come in," said Mother, "and make yourself at
home." **6.** inferior. **7.** (a) infrequent; (b) inexpensive. **8.** lamb. **9.** Mary *said*
she could *have* killed him. **10.** (a) picturesque; (b) mosque, etc. **11.** sworn,
took. **12.** (a) unimportant; (b) interior. **13.** "Is there any room for me?"
asked John. **14.** footwear. **15.** barbarian. **16.** (*b*). **17.** The buses that go to
Beyton and back pass our door frequently. **18.** Permission to go home gave (great)
relief to the boys.

TEST 22

A

1. On the River Thames. 2. City, West End, Westminster, central business area. 3. Westminster 4. Soho. 5. Oxford Street and Regent Street. 6. Westminster. 7. a small part. 8. the city of London. 9. the West End. 10. Westminster.

B

1. (a) sign; (b) signature. 2. league. 3. Dickory Dock. 4. Who's. 5. "I never said I didn't," said Alice. / "You did," said the Mock Turtle. 6. (a) Patrick; (b) Daniel; (c) Edward. 7. fortify. 8. (a) calf; (b) sheep; (c) pig. 9. It was I who broke the window. 10. (a) circular; (b) circulation. 11. rang. 12. (a) disconnect; (b) undo. 13. "I shall be going to London tomorrow." 14. (a) On Her Majesty's Service; (b) Justice of the Peace; (c) United States of America. 15. benefit. 16. (c). 17. This is my favourite desk at which I do most of my writing. 18. Tom's pride prevented us from liking him.

TEST 23

A

1. five: monkey, cow, donkey, elephant, goat. 2. the cow. 3. three. 4. the friend of the man who owns the donkey. 5. "sneak." 6. the man on the elephant; a turban. 7. to and fro. 8. "huge strides." 9. the owner of the donkey. 10. (a) tit-bit; (b) morsels.

B

1. written. 2. Shall we play Blind Man's Buff? 3. (a) delicate; (b) fragile; (c) frail. 4. its. 5. "How do you know I'm mad?" said Alice. / "You must be," said the Cat, "or you wouldn't come here." 6. Susan, Margaret, Violet, Diana. 7. cereals. 8. deer. 9. He and I . . . 10. studious. 11. I ran after the thief and caught him . . . 12. (a) invisible; (b) discourteous. 13. "My ship will remain in the bay." 14. liquids. 15. margin. 16. (c). 17. Mary is a good friend with whom I spend many happy hours. 18. The glare of the headlights prevented us from seeing their faces.

TEST 24

A

1. 850 years. 2. River Thames. 3. abruptly. 4. Buckingham Palace, Sandringham House, etc. 5. Nine. 6. restorations. 7. Architect. 8. cloisters. 9. Fifteenth. 10. Curfew bell. 11. The dungeon. 12. Elizabeth II (or the Second).

B

1. draughty. 2. zinc. 3. Little Boy Blue, come, blow me your horn. 4. Will (you) not. 5. "Hold your tongue," said the Queen, turning purple. / "I won't," said Alice. / "Off with her head," the Queen shouted at the top of her voice. 6. James, Samuel, Robert. 7. glaze. 8. (a) caddy; (b) chest. 9. These shoes have worn out quickly. 10. enrich. 11. known, what, hidden. 12. (a) useless; (b) displace. 13. "I am glad to see you." 14. Atlas. 15. breach. 16. (c). 17. A man who was looking for his wife knocked at our door. 18. The departure of the visitors will be (is timed for) (will take place at) noon tomorrow.

TEST 25

A

1. creature, beast. 2. to save himself. 3. He hadn't time to climb a tree. 4. The bear thought the man was dead. 5. He lay still and did not breathe. 6. companion. 7. "leave their friends in the lurch." 8. because he was safe. 9. that he had seen the bear whisper to his friend. 10. (c).

B

1. January, February, August. 2. does. 3. Little Jack Horner / Sat in a corner / Eating his Christmas pie. 4. ladies'. 5. "How many sweets," asked Tom, "shall I get for 5p?" / "Oh, six or seven," said the shopkeeper. / "Then I'll have seven," said Tom. 6. Alexander, Richard, Thomas. 7. selvedge. 8. microscope. 9. swam, swum. 10. wearily. 11. nor, are. 12. disallowed. 13. "I haven't seen you for a long time." 14. telephone directory. 15. parapet. 16. (c). 17. Jones who had received the ball from Brown passed it to Smith who was waiting on the right wing. 18. The decision of the committee was to resign.

TEST 26

A

1. surnames. 2. very small villages. 3. sire-names (or family names), trade names and place names. 4. father. 5. everyone knew everyone else and a surname was not needed. 6. A.D. 1066. 7. ancestors. 8. four: John, Stephen, Hugh, Walter. 9. four: Baker, Miller, Tailor, Tyler. 10. "practically all."

B

1. carriage; marriage. 2. lamb, cygnets, eaglets, goslings. 3. Little Miss Muffett / Sat on a tuffet / Eating her curds and whey. 4. Tom's, Mary's. 5. "Now, Sam," said Mr. Pickwick, "the first thing to be done is to order dinner." / "Sir," interposed Sam. 6. Elizabeth, Joseph, Florence, Pamela. 7. pilgrim. 8. telescope (field glasses). 9. rung, rang. 10. befriended. 11. who, come. 12. immortal. 13. The little boy said that he had lost his mother. 14. album. 15. byways. 16. (d). 17. The dog chased the cat which he saw in the garden. 18. The grace and elegance of the skater in all she did thrilled the spectators.

TEST 27

A

1. marking the path. 2. master. 3. occasionally. 4. set fire to. 5. five. 6. find his way back. 7. axe, hatchet. 8. peas. 9. coconut trees. 10. coconut grove.

B

1. receipt. 2. (a) filleting; (b) fumigating. 3. My favourite English king is Alfred. 4. I should, women's. 5. "Stop," said Mr Pickwick. / "What now?" said Wardle. 6. (a) mare and foal; (b) cow and heifer. 7. legible. 8. (a) oaks; (b) palms; (c) chestnuts. 9. drank, drunk. 10. graze. 11. queue. 12. illogical. 13. "I will never send you away." 14. astronomy. 15. caution. 16. (d). 17. This is Tom Burns with whom I sometimes go fishing. 18. The chance of your winning is small (remote).

Published in 1984 by Bell & Hyman Limited,
Denmark House, 37–39 Queen Elizabeth Street,
London SE1 2QB

First published in 1961 by Evans Brothers Limited
Sixteenth printing 1984

© Bell & Hyman Limited 1984

All rights reserved. No part of this publication may
be reproduced, stored in a retrieval system, or
transmitted, in any form or by any means, electronic,
mechanical, photocopying, recording or otherwise,
without the prior permission of Bell & Hyman Limited.

Printed in Great Britain at
The Camelot Press Ltd, Southampton
ISBN 0 7135 2402 2